The Place Na~~~~~~a

by Joan Lee

HS Heritage Services

Cumbria

COUNTY COUNCIL

This edition first published in England 1998 by
Cumbria Heritage Services, Arroyo, The Castle,
Carlisle CA3 8UR

Copyright © Joan Lee, 1998

The author has asserted her moral rights

A CIP catalogue record for this book is available
from the British Library
ISBN 0 905404 70 X

Printed in Great Britain by Manchester Free Press,
Longford Trading Estate, Thomas Street, Stretford,
M32 0JT

Foreword

So, "what's in a name?" It has been said, with some justification, that place names are signposts to the past and nowhere is this better exemplified than in Cumbria. Settled and colonized by Celts and Anglians, by Danes, Irish-Norse and Normans, the place name maps of the county tell their own fascinating story.

The elements *glen*, a valley, and *pen*, a hill, still to be found in Wales, are distant echoes of the indigenous British people; the *-ton* and *-ham* endings speak of the Anglian farmers who cultivated the fertile soils of the Eden Valley, the West Cumbrian plain and Low Furness, while the *thwaites, fells, forces,* and *becks* of our Norse ancestors bristle on the current map of the Lake District as they do on modern maps of Norway.

In short, those nameless men and women who tilled the land, felled the forest, herded their sheep, pigs, and cattle, and created a network of fields, hamlets, and villages also stamped their characteristic place names on mountain and moorland, fell and forest, lake and lowland for later generations to read and decipher.

Joan Lee's delightful and diligent survey of Cumbria's place names provides us with the means to interpret that landscape; it will appeal to the curious traveller intrigued by the names on signposts, to the student of both history and geography, to the casual tourist, to offcomer and native alike - indeed, to all those who know and love this most beautiful part of north west England.

William Rollinson

Acknowledgements

I am indebted to my husband, Jerry, who tirelessly and uncomplainingly put this work onto the computer. He accompanied me on many fact-finding trips to Cumbria and shared my enthusiasm during the research.

My thanks go to our son Jonathan who arranged for the drawings to be scanned by Rodger Keegan and for copying the text; also to Karen Knowles, an expert computer animator, who kindly turned hand drawn maps into professional computerised images.

The artist is our daughter Susie Lee, who trained at Dartington College in Devon. She has held three exhibitions of her work in Oman, India, and London. She is an Assistant Art Director in the film industry, based in London.

A debt of gratitude is owing to a friend, Michael Morris, who selflessly verified certain facts in the London Library.

Finally I give grateful thanks to Dr. William Rollinson for writing the foreword to this book. His knowledge of the history, geography, dialect and folklore of Cumbria is second to none. He has been most encouraging, helpful and supportive.

Preface

I have been asked frequently how I set about my research for this book, but never why. The interest shown by everybody when I talk about it proves the fascination the subject has. The question everyone poses is how I have reached solutions when there is scant early literature or obvious evidence to go on.

In 1961 I presented a thesis for my degree in English Language. This was entitled "Scandinavian Elements in North West Place-Names" which triggered my love of the subject and which I used as a source and basis for this book.

A second source was The English Place-Name Society which has catalogued practically all the early forms of the Cumbrian place-names from parish registers, old documents, Furness Abbey records and the like.

It is well known that the earliest land survey, Domesday Book, 1086, hardly touches Cumbria, and what names were noted, were recorded under Yorkshire. It seems likely that Domesday surveyors never ventured north of the Kent estuary and made a guess as to where, for example, Hougun was, a fairly important place occupied by Earl Tostig, now thought to be the Furness peninsula.

The recorded early forms of place-names, whilst very important, merely show their pronunciation as perceived by scribes at the time. It is obvious that some names are much older, by sometimes as much as 600 years and possibly 1000 years, than the version heard and recorded in the 11th or 12th centuries. Some places also had begun as one name in one language and had been altered to suit the language of subsequent inhabitants; examples are Walney and Ravenglass.

All place-name researchers try to reach back as far as possible to discover the original meaning of a name and I have made some new discoveries.

One name which proves to be much older than previously thought, is Cartmel. Other place-name investigators, the most important being Eilert Ekwall, assumed Cartmel was Norse in origin and meant 'sandbank in rough ground'. However this name was mentioned by Camden in his Britannia and I quote in a translation from his original Latin, in 677, "Egfrid, King of Northumbria, gave to St. Cuthbert the land of Cartmel, and all the Britons in it...so it says in his life". This was at least 200 years before the Norse came to Cumbria, so the name could not possibly be Norse. As a child travelling on the train from Preston to my home town Barrow I remember hearing the stationmaster call out "Cark and Cartmel!", and because of his pronunciation I thought one was an extension of the other, and indeed this is likely to be so linguistically. If it is assumed that the place-name dates from the 5th or 6th century, then its origin would be in the British language of the time, and so the first element of Cartmel is of the same origin as Cark from Celtic carrec 'rock' and the second element is moel 'hill'. The main feature of Cartmel is the weathered limestone hill now known as Hampsfield Fell immediately east of the village. This is the rocky hill of the name. There is no evidence of any sand dunes or sand deposits in the area.

There are many hill names in Cumbria from the Celtic moel such as the second element of Cartmel and Great Mell Fell. There are also several with the name Bell such as Ill Bell and Cat Bells. It is possible that this element is from Old Norse belja 'bell or bell-shaped', but could there be a connection between mell and bell? It is known that the initial 'b' in early Celtic could become 'm' under certain circumstances, but could the reverse be true? The Celtic specialists I asked were unable to answer, but if it were true, many more names could be of earlier, Celtic, origin than had been supposed.

It seems likely that a word like Duddon, explained by Ekwall and others as Duðn's valley, was much older than Norse. As other names in the Duddon Valley show a strong British presence (Penn, Wallowbarrow), it is certain that the name of the river, a strong deep clear river, must be Celtic as indeed most rivers are in Britain. This is where an invaluable booklet published by the Ordnance Survey 'Place names on maps of Scotland and Wales' comes in, and from which I have gleaned much information. Duddon remains a mystery but it is possible it could mean 'deep river' from the Celtic words dufn and afon, the elements being presented under the Welsh glossary. Blen Cathra's elements, blaen 'mountain' and cathair 'seat', 'chair', or 'circular stone fort' were in the Scottish list.

Other new suggestions and interpretations on the place-names of Cumbria have come to light during the research for this book. I am not certain that they are foolproof, but they are worth serious consideration. On realising that the Celtic word ar 'on the' is used as a first element as in Arlecdon, I extended it to other names hitherto unexplained, as Arrow, Arrad, and eventually Arthur as in Arthur's Seat. Little Arrow Moor near Coniston has many ancient remains, tumuli, and stone circles, some of which have been excavated. There is a Celtic word 'rhiw' meaning a hillside, and I have assumed that Ar rhiw 'on the hillside', becomes Arrow (although the dative singular of ON erg 'at the shieling' could be the explanation of this name). Ar ardd 'on the high point' becomes Arrad. Ar torr 'on the hill' becomes Arthur, spelt this way no doubt because of the medieval fascination with King Arthur. 'Seat' would be Old Norse saetr 'summer shieling', added to the original Celtic name.

Peter Berresford Ellis in his various excellent books on the Celts, suggests the name maiden, as in Maiden Castle, the name of an Iron Age hill fort in Dorset and now extended to many defended prehistoric sites, could mean 'Maia's fort', the second element being Celtic dun 'fort'. I suggest the first element could be Celtic meini, plural of maen, 'stones'. Maiden Moor is the name of the mountain near Keswick. Could it have had a stone fort on top as did Carrock Fell? Investigation proved nothing, except that the summit was a likely spot for such a fort, with a broad rocky knoll defended naturally on one side by a vertical drop.

It is always worthwhile visiting a place if there is any doubt of the meaning of the name. 'Crook' has always been assumed to mean 'bend in the river' from Old Norse krokr. This is true in some cases but not all. A visit to the hamlet of Crook near Kendal shows the stream there to be straight and not large enough to have had an impact on the name. But there is a steep hill on leaving the village to the west, and there is a Celtic word 'cruc' meaning a hill, so that seems to be the more likely explanation in this case. Further to the east in the county there is another Crook actually referring to a hill.

Places containing the element 'ro' as in Roa Island, Roanhead, and Rowe Head exhibit red ground from iron ore, so it can be assumed the element is from Old Norse rauðr 'red'. Not so the river Rothay however which is not running over a sandstone bed, nor could be named after red trout which was suggested by Ekwall. Its name means 'loud sounding' from a Norse present participle of a verb meaning to be noisy and indeed the answer lies at your feet when you are there.

By far the most interesting question raised by this research is the meaning of the word 'kirk'. Usually it is from Old Norse kirkja adapted from Old English cirice and means a church, and the word survives as such in Scotland. However on reading a book on the stone circles of Cumbria by John Waterhouse I became aware that many of them had the word kirk in their names. Kirk on its own is the name of a circular homestead on Kirkby Moor, with no church nearby nor would a church ever have been built here, which happened sometimes when the early Christians were trying to diffuse the power of ancient stone circles. Kirkstone Pass was examined carefully and it is possible that there was a circle on the summit though the litter and debris fallen from the heights above for over 3000 years makes it difficult to be sure. There is a circle at Hird Wood about a mile south east of the summit.

If Kirksanton near Millom could at one point have been Kirkstanton (and there were three stone circles here, one of which was named Kirkstones) the name would mean 'farm at the stone circle'. Interestingly, in a discussion on this very name, W.J. Sedgefield in his 'Place-names of Cumberland and Westmorland' in 1915 includes a quotation from the Reverend James Wilson, the editor of 'The Victoria History of Cumberland': 'I think that Santacherche, Kirksanton, Chapel Sucken, and Sunken Kirk (a megalithic circle) are all variants of the same idea'. As far as I know, this is the only record of a reference to 'kirk' meaning a circle. However Sanctan is an Irish saint's name and 'Sanctan's church' is a plausible meaning for Kirksanton, though there is no church in this village now.

Kirk Fell in Wasdale has an unusually regular conical shape, and it seems likely that 'circle mountain' is a good descriptive name.

On a map of the Yorkshire Dales I noticed near Casterton the name Ease Gill Kirk referring to a circular chamber in the river bed. There is an Upper Kirk on the same river.

In the Oxford Dictionary of Etymology the explanation of circle says that Old French 'cercle' replaced an earlier Old English word 'circul' from Latin circulus. How this word would have been pronounced is important. If it retained the hard 'c', then some of the names with kirk could be Old English (the unstressed second element dying away). If the 'c' was softened to 'ch', then another influence on the word would have had to have been exerted, namely Norse. Some Old English words are known to have been Scandinavianised (see Keswick).

So my theory is that when the Norse came to Cumbria in the 10th century, they adopted the Old English word 'circul' meaning (stone) circle, hardening the initial 'c' to suit their own tongue, unless it was already hard, there being no word for circle in their own language.

This is probably impossible to prove. However as Professor Mills of Liverpool University pointed out when I put this idea to him, the word kirk was used in the 14th century story of Sir Gawain and the Green Knight, 'the corsedest kyrk that ever I com inne', to refer to a mound at the green chapel. Could this be the last reference to kirk meaning circle before it sank into obscurity? Maybe the author of Gawain used the word as a pun, with the double meaning 'church' and 'circle'. The story is thought to have been set in the north west of England.

The English Place-Name Society Volume 3 cites 'kirk' as meaning church and a pile of stones, so they agree that there are two interpretations of the word, though do not go as far as defining it as I have.

The word 'wheel' from Old English hweol or hwerfel, or ON hjol, is also used in Cumbria and other parts of the country to denote a circle, but no evidence has been found of 'ring', which seems to be confined to the south of England.

Cumbria is unique in its place-names. Nowhere else in Britain shows evidence of such a diversity of influences - both types of Celtic, Brythonic and Goedelic, Roman, Anglian, Irish, Norse, Danish and Norman. Norse is by far the largest influence with a strong substructure of Celtic.

The aim of this book is to provide an easily accessible dictionary of the meanings of the place-names of this most beautiful and distinctive part of England, for tourists, students and interested local people, without being too academic or pedantic. With local knowledge, I have challenged some previous explanations in a sincere attempt to extend understanding of the history of Cumbria. All the names listed, apart from lost or historic names, such as Hougun and Rheged, are to be found on the Ordnance Survey Landranger series maps, numbers 85, 86, 89, 90, 91, 96 and 97.

The dictionary is by no means exhaustive, and the research and exploration continue.

Old road junction at Longlands Farm, near Cartmel

Introduction

Cumbria is a large county in north west England, formed in 1974 by an amalgamation of Cumberland, Westmorland and part of Lancashire. Its boundaries are Scotland to the north, the Pennines and counties of Northumberland, Durham and North Yorkshire to the east, Lancashire to the south and the Irish Sea to the west.

The landscape, which is as varied as the place-names, is unique. The central portion of Cumbria is the Lake District National Park, probably one of the most beautiful areas in the world with its majestic mountains, calm clear lakes, tumbling waterfalls and pretty villages. It has been well documented, painted and explored. The surrounding areas, which make up the rest of Cumbria, are less well known.

The Furness peninsula, with its islands of Walney, Roa, Foulney and Piel, has a quiet charm. The rich haematite deposits here were exploited from early times. An Iron Age bloomery has been found on the north end of Walney, and iron ore was probably exported from Roa. The 12th century Furness Abbey, now well-preserved ruins in the 'vale of the deadly nightshade' was a most important administrative centre in the early middle ages, and held control of much of south west Cumbria.

The coastal strip to the west is peppered with evidence of early settlers. The modern nuclear power station of Sellafield has been built next to a Bronze Age stone circle. The port of Ravenglass, now largely silted up, was of great importance to the Romans, who had a fort here, but was more than likely to have been used by previous incomers.

The flat fertile plain to the north west of Cumbria has been continuously inhabited by Britons, Romans, Scots, Irish, Anglians, Danes and Normans. The important county town of Carlisle has a long and chequered history and has been destroyed and rebuilt many times. Hadrians Wall ran through it, and most Roman roads at the time led to it.

The north east of the county, a large limestone tract from Shap to Appleby, shows much early occupation in the form of settlements, stone circles, tumuli, and earthworks. It is thought to have been the centre of the 6th century kingdom of Rheged, ruled by Urien, a forceful leader believed by some to have been the model for King Arthur. The broad and fertile Eden Valley was used as a corridor between east and west Britain from early times, and its many castles of varying ages point to its strategic importance.

To the east of the M6 lie the Howgills, such different mountains from the Lakeland fells to the west. Garsdale and Dentdale are actually part of the Yorkshire Dales National Park, yet are in Cumbria. In this region on top of several hills are found 'men' or 'standards', unexplained neatly built tall cairns, singly or in groups, possibly used as primitive signposts to early travellers, or boundary marks.

The limestone outcrops of Cartmel and Silverdale, bisected by the estuary of the river Kent are most attractive areas and again show evidence of early occupation. The priory at Cartmel, although smaller than Furness Abbey, played a similar role of local management during the Middle Ages.

With its hundreds of miles of public footpaths and rights of way, Cumbria can provide years of fascinating discovery. The study of the place-names is linguistic archaeology and unveils the layers of humanity who have dwelt there.

Stone Age

Stone Age Cumbria would have had a very different landscape from the pastorally farmed 18th-19th century setting. The valley floors would have been swampy and impenetrable, and the hills covered in trees, probably birch, oak, rowan, ash and fir. Place-names like Cat Bells show that wild cats abounded, and Ulpha and Latterbarrow that there were wolves.

There are three large stone circles attributed to the New Stone Age: at Swinside near Millom, Long Meg and her Daughters at Little Salkeld north east of Penrith, and at Castlerigg outside Keswick, near which it is possible there was a Stone Age village at Portinscale. There were more megalithic circles which have now all but disappeared, removed for agricultural purposes or the stones purloined for buildings or walls. These are Grey Yauds in the north east of Cumbria, Gamelands and Rawthey Bridge in the east, Motherby and Elva Plain in the north, and several in the south west quadrant at Hall Foss, and Annaside. The three at Kirksanton, may have caused the place to be named 'farm at the stone circle' - in fact one of the circles was named Kirkstones.

There seem to be no other place-names attached to these important rings, nor of other Neolithic finds, such as the burial mound on Sizergh Fell, the Giant's Grave in Woodland or the signs of occupation round Gibb Tarn, Ehenside, on the western coast.

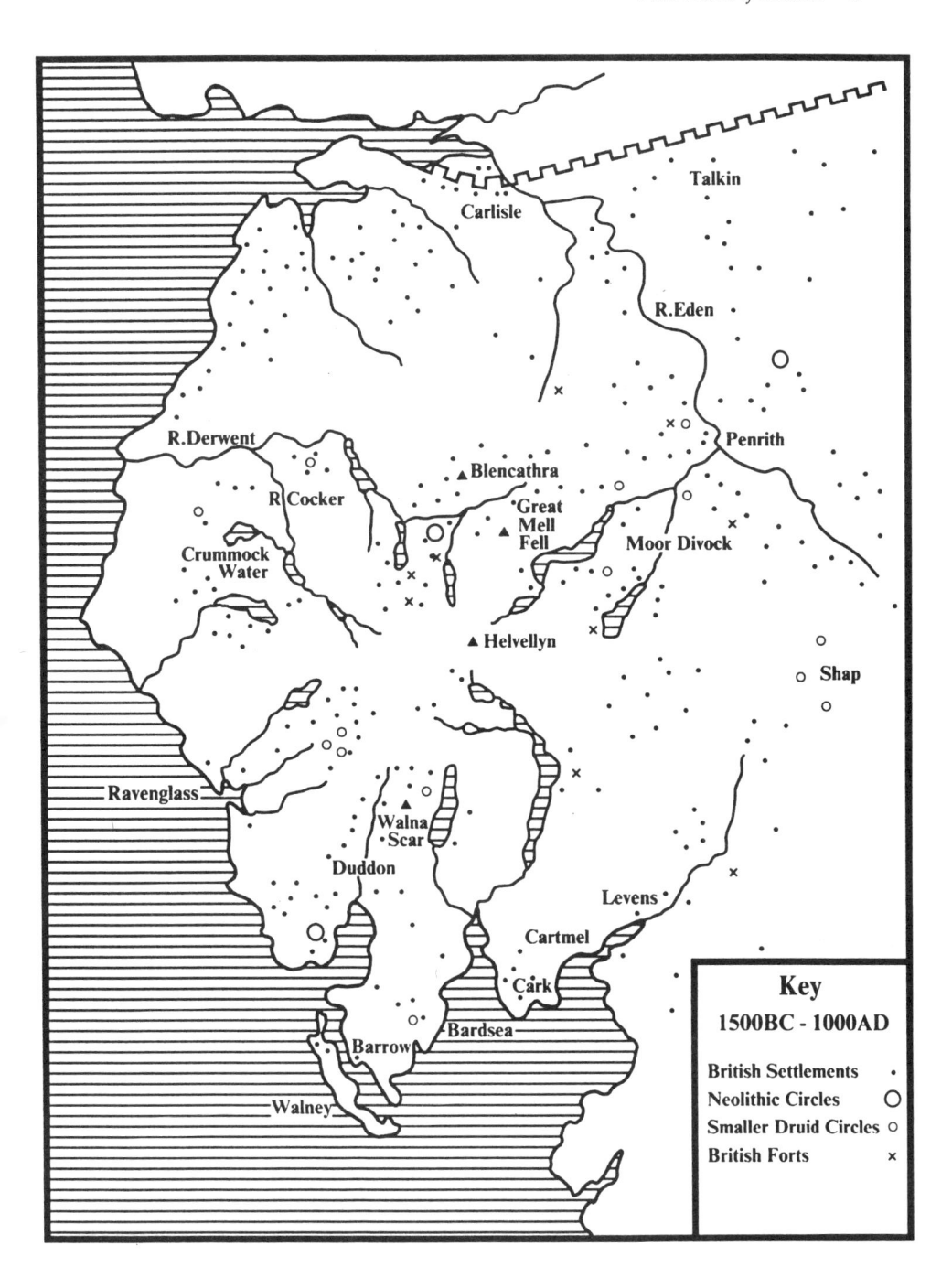

Place Names of Cumbria ix

Key
1500BC - 1000AD

British Settlements •
Neolithic Circles ◯
Smaller Druid Circles ○
British Forts ×

There are many standing stones and smaller circles of Bronze Age origin in Cumbria, nearly all on land of about 1000 feet above sea level around Black Combe, Coniston, Keswick, and Penrith. These are noted by later inhabitants in their place-names, such as Quarles, Shap, and Whillimoor by the Anglians, Shoulthwaite and possibly Kirk by the Norse.

The word cairn is from Celtic carn and means a pile of stones. Cumbria is well known for its cairns, which can mark the summit of a fell, a route, or an ancient grave. The word 'man', from Celtic maen, also means a stone and is often used to mean a standing stone or a cairn. The Norse named cairns 'raise' from hreysi, Dunmail Raise being the most well known.

The name Borran is found frequently throughout Cumbria in various forms such as Barn-, Burn-, Borwen, and denotes ancient remains found by Anglians from their word 'borgaesn'. Even the Roman fort at the head of Windermere is in Borran Field. Similarly, the name Birrel or Burrels is from Old English burgaels and means a burial place. Occasionally a Burrels Hill is found next to an ancient settlement.

It is difficult to put a date on these remains. The Iron Age in southern England became established much sooner than in Cumbria, so what is thought of as Iron Age in chronological terms could still have been theoretically late Bronze Age in the north west.

The British

In the Iron Age there were British settlements, villages of a primitive type such as those at Kentmere, Urswick and Lanthwaite Green near Crummock. The most extensive are at Barnscar and Burnmoor in the western area of Cumbria, and the Crosby Ravensworth district near Shap, but there is some evidence to show that these were of an even earlier date. Hill forts on Carrock Fell, at Peel Wyke on Bassenthwaite, Tilberthwaite, and the many Castle Crags, Castle Hows, and Castle Heads scattered throughout the region lend weight to the belief that they were places where the Britons took refuge from invaders during the Roman period, the Scots during the 4th century, and the Vikings in the 9th century. Castle, which appears in Celtic as castell, and in Anglo-Norman as castle, is from Latin castellum, meaning a fortified stronghold. Caer, as in the first element of Carlisle, is a British word for fort. Many hill and mountain names, such as Mell, Pen, Blen, and rivers such as Eden, Kent, Derwent, and Leven, are British, as are Cark and Cartmel. It seems that names like Duddon and Ravenglass are British in origin, remodelled by Norse hundreds of years later.

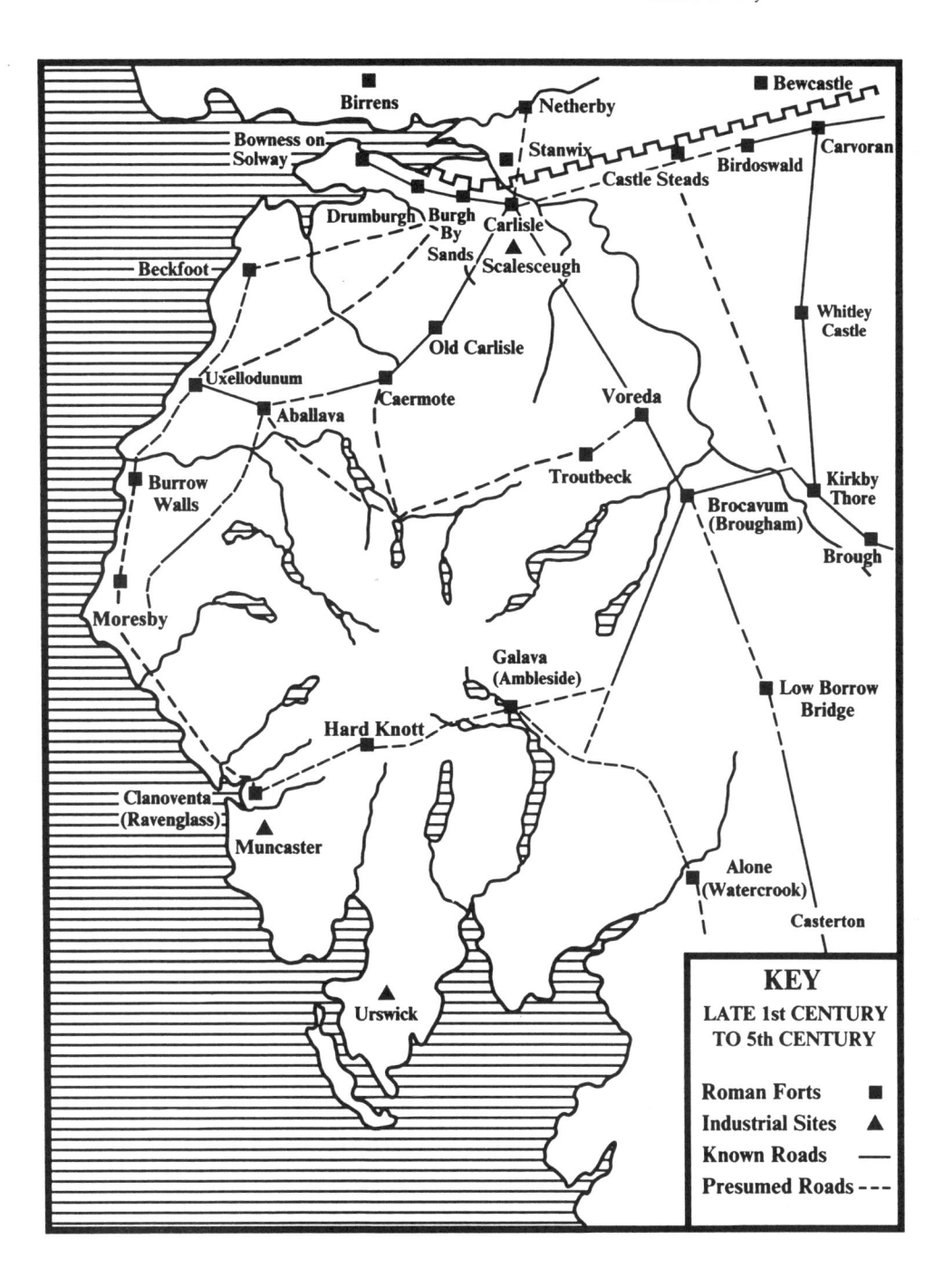

Place Names of Cumbria xi

That groups of British people still remained in the Norse era, that is from the 10th to 12th centuries, is evidenced by the Scandinavian place-names Brettargh near Sizergh Castle, and Birkby near Maryport, the early form of which Bretteby, shows it to mean 'home of the Britons'. Walla Crag, Walna Scar, and Wallowbarrow show either OE wealh or ON valr as the first element, meaning 'hill of the British'.

The Romans

The Romans arrived in Cumbria towards the end of the first century AD. All place-names containing the word caster from the Latin castellum as in Muncaster were Roman forts, as were Burgh by Sands and Stanwix on Hadrian's Wall. Some words ending in wick, as in Keswick and Urswick show an early Latin loan word vicus meaning 'village' which becomes OE wic, pronounced with a hard 'c' in Northern England, probably because of the Scandinavian influence. Indeed the first element of Urswick could be Latin aes 'ore'.

Most of the names ending in 'wick' (from vicus) in Cumbria are on known Roman roads, and a case can be made for all the others to be too. The Romans established forts at Hard Knott and Ambleside. Only one of the original Roman names survives, which is Brougham from Brocavum, otherwise Ravenglass, which they used as a harbour was Clanoventa, the Ambleside fort was Galava, Voreda was a habitation near Penrith, and Aballava near Cockermouth. The second element of Carlisle is reputedly from a Romano-British name Luguvallus.

A Roman road ran from Ravenglass up Eskdale to Hard Knott, which was linked to Ambleside probably by the present road over Wrynose Pass. This road continued up Troutbeck, visible to this day cutting diagonally across the Yoke, Ill Bell, and Froswick range, over High Street, which mountain is named after it, and onto Brougham in the Eden Valley. Another road ran south from Ambleside towards present day Kendal and down the Kent valley to join the Lancaster to Ribchester road. It does not appear to have originated any names of places along the way. There are likely to be more Roman roads in Cumbria than has previously been thought. The modern roads in the north of the county, such as the A595 from Papcastle, or the A596 from Workington to Carlisle, are arrow straight and obviously of Roman origin.

The Romans were fond of horse racing, as were the Norse as evidenced by place-names such as Hesketh and Hesket. There was a race-course probably used by the Romans, on High Street, which bears the modern name Racecourse Hill.

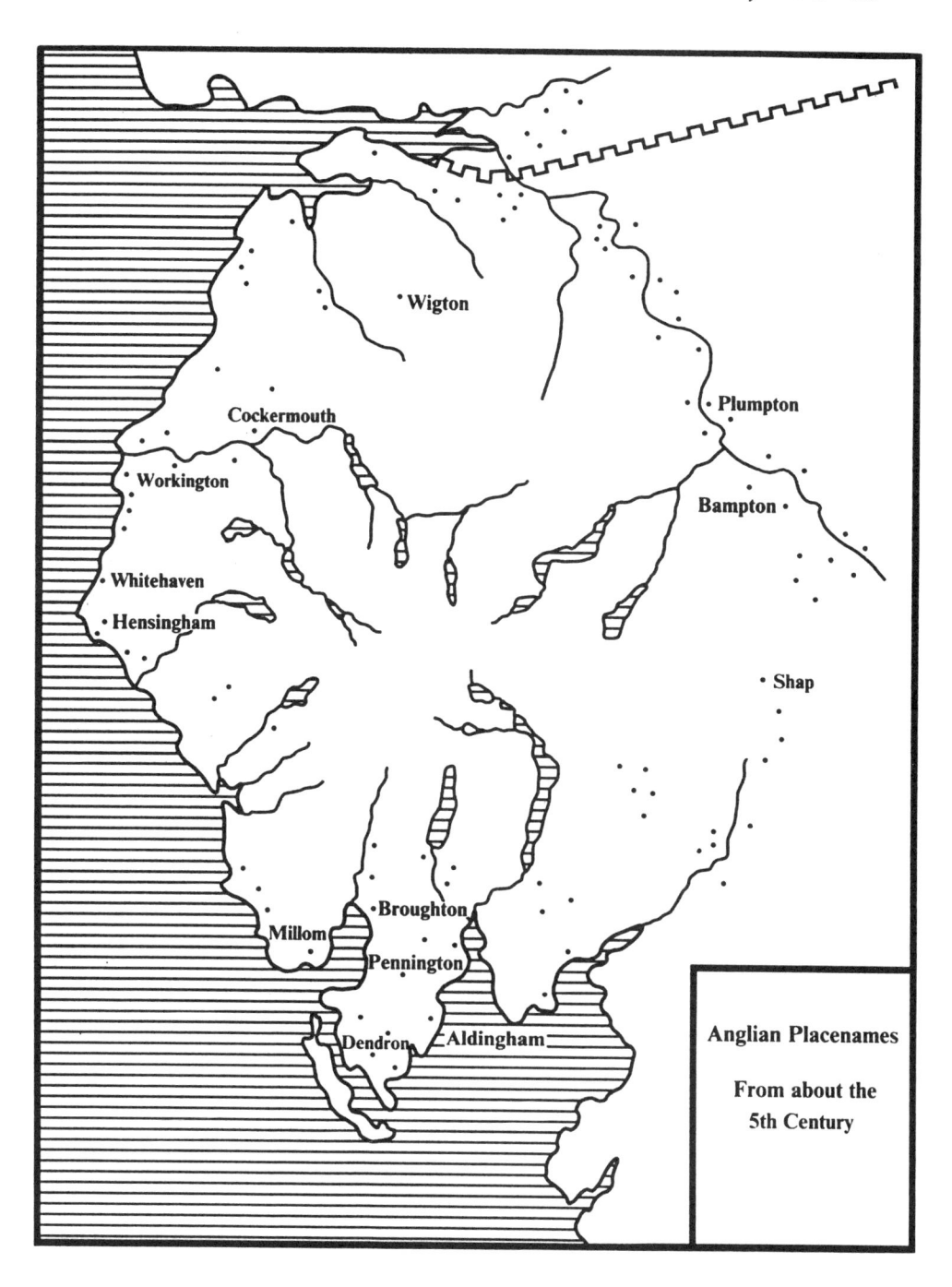

Place Names of Cumbria xiii

Anglian Placenames

From about the 5th Century

The Anglo Saxons

Angles from Deira north of the Humber filtered into Cumbria, probably between the 5th and 8th centuries, along the then undefended Hadrian's Wall and certainly through the Stainmore Pass to the Eden valley as is shown by the name Inglewood 'wood of the Angles'. They tended to stay in the fertile lowland areas along the coast as is shown by names such as Wigton and Workington. Also in this area are several place-names of Danish origin like Thursby and Motherby suggesting the movement of Danes from eastern England along the same routes.

In 685 AD St. Cuthbert, Bishop of Lindisfarne, came to Carlisle and founded a monastery here. He had already been given 'Cartmel and all the Britons around it' and now his see was endowed with an extensive estate which included Carlisle. Probably slightly later Anglo-Saxons, crossing from the east of England via Skipton, settled in the low Furness peninsula and formed villages called Aldingham, Broughton, Dendron, and Pennington, (though the first element of this name could have been the British word penaig 'prince or chieftain'. See under Pennington).

It appears from place-name evidence that the Anglo-Saxons did not venture into the high mountainous area, except for hermits like St. Herbert, who lived in isolation on an island in Derwentwater, which still bears his name.

The Norse

From about 925AD Norwegians started arriving by boat from Iceland, the Hebrides, Ireland and the Isle of Man which they had already colonised. These were peaceful invaders looking for land in which to settle unlike the warring Danes who had harried the east coast of England, burning and looting more than a century before. They would probably have arrived in small groups, sometimes with Irish wives and servants as is shown by several place-names such as Ireby, Ireleth, and Threlkeld.

Irish saints like Sancton, Oswald and Patrick are remembered in place-names such as Kirksanton, Kirkoswald, and Patterdale. There is evidence of Irish priests as in Papcastle. One of the greatest Irish influences on the naming of places was the inversion of the elements where the descriptive word appears second, such as Aspatria, Brigsteer, and Kirby Stephen. These so-called inversion compounds are a feature of the other branch of Celtic, known as Goidelic, existing still in

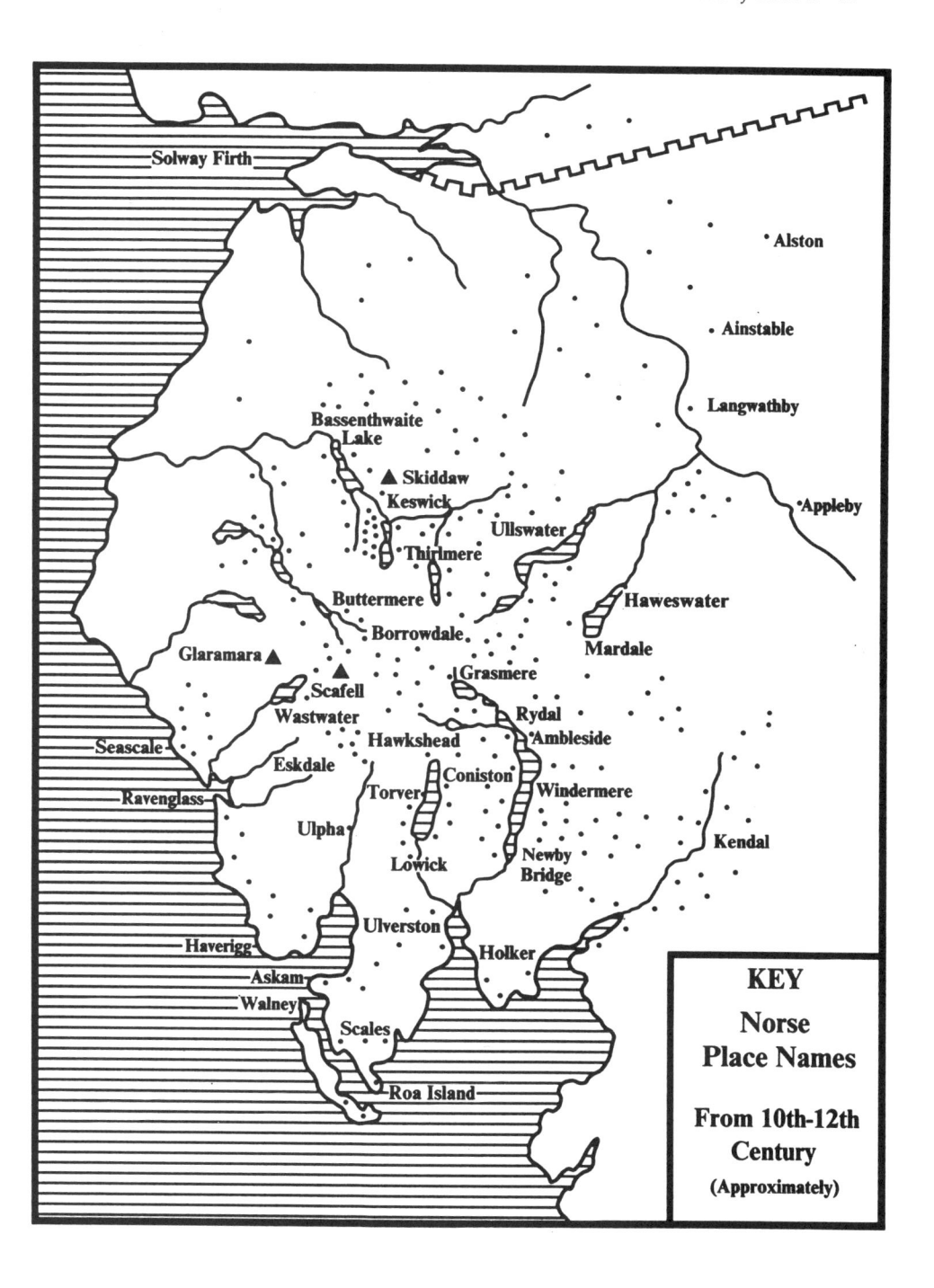

Place Names of Cumbria xv

KEY

Norse Place Names

From 10th-12th Century

(Approximately)

Ireland, Man and Scotland, as opposed to Brythonic (British) which survives in Welsh, Cornish and Breton.

The legacy of the Norsemen is enormous. Most of the place-names in the Cumbria National Park are of Old Norse origin, and names such as Rusland and Laufvik (Lowick) are also found in Scandinavian countries.

The Place-names

To have a good guide to the origin of the meaning of place-names it is essential to have early recorded forms of the words. These however tell you no more about the name than how it was pronounced at the time of writing, the sounds heard by the chronicler and sometimes 'corrected' to make sense. For example Ravenglass recorded as such in 1297 was earlier recorded as Rengles in 1170, which would point to a Celtic origin such as Reannaglas 'river with promontories'. Sometimes words like 'fell' were added to an original 'mell' which already meant hill. Indeed Pendle Hill in Lancashire has three meanings of hill, 'pen' in British, 'hlaw' in Old English and 'hill' in Modern English.

After the Norman Conquest in 1066, Domesday Book was commissioned by William I and twenty years later was completed. It was a survey of all English land and the revenues likely from the occupiers. Domesday Book was the first notable recording of place-names which had the effect of fixing them and slowing down their development. Apart from Furness, which was known as Hougun, Cumbria is not covered. A century later though, organisation and cataloguing by abbeys such as Furness and Calder, the priories of Conishead and Cartmel and various parish churches give the records which can be used as guides to the origin of most of the place-names of Cumbria.

Place-names are usually in two parts, or elements, although there are some names such as Frith and Storth which have only one, and others like Tilberthwaite, Watendlath and Legburthwaite which are made up of three.

The first element is often a personal name, such as Ulfarr in Ulverston, or Arni in Arnside, an adjective, such as groenn in Greenodd, or austr 'east' in Austhwaite, or a common noun, such as gris 'pig' in Grisedale, birkr 'birch tree' in Birkrigg and hros 'horse' in Rosthwaite.

The second elements are very often Norse, 'dale' from dalr, 'rig' from hryggr, 'ghyll' from gil, 'how' from haugr, 'fell' from fjallr, 'beck' from bekkr, 'tarn' from

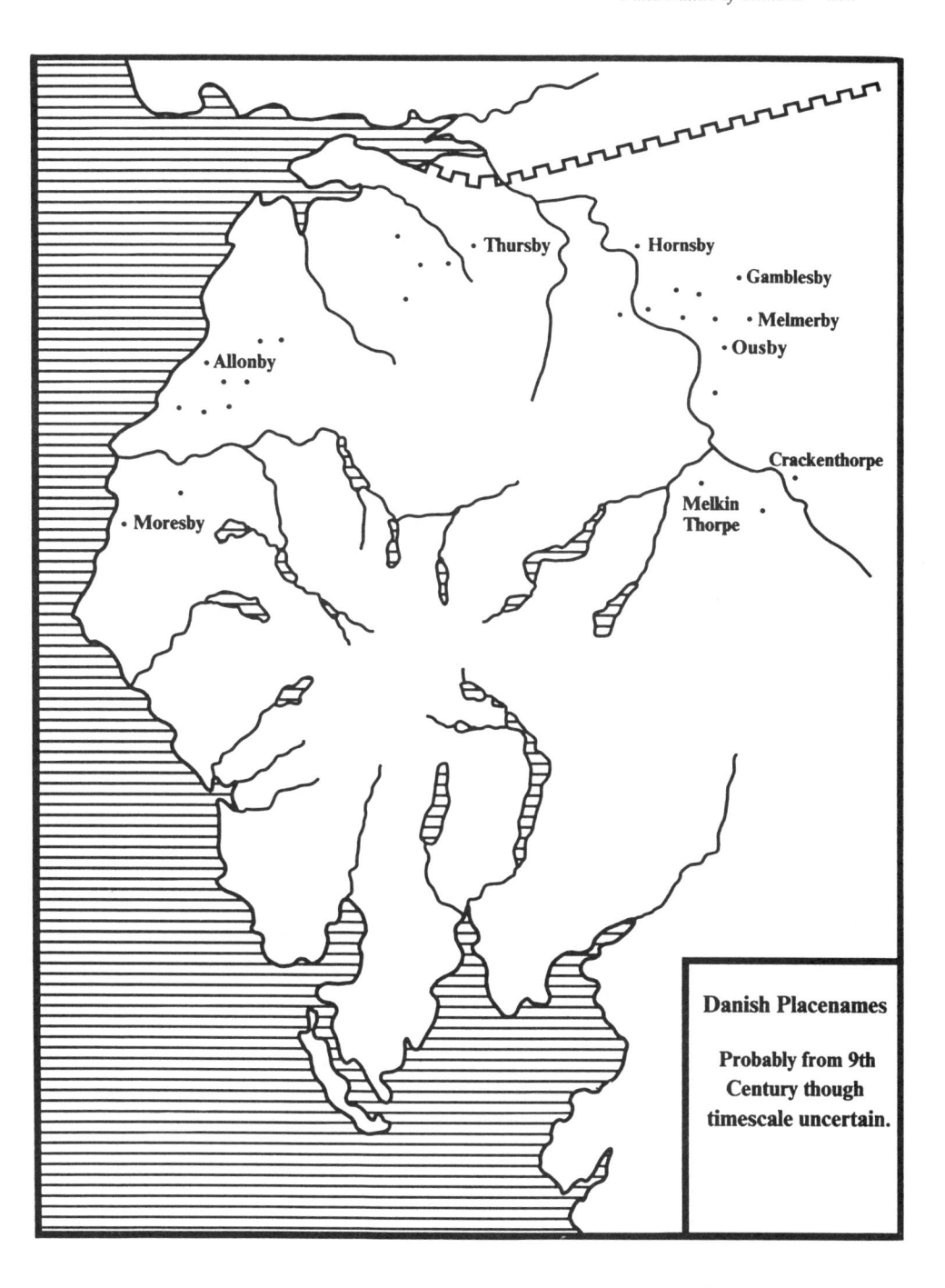

Place Names of Cumbria xvii

Danish Placenames

Probably from 9th Century though timescale uncertain.

tjorn and 'force' from fors. Some could be either Old English or Old Norse, like 'land', 'ness', 'moss', and 'syke'. There are many second elements denoting dwelling places or shelters of some kind. 'Scale', 'booth', and '-set' or '-side' meaning a shieling, are mainly summer huts, as the practice was usual of moving sheep and cattle to different grazing areas higher up the fells in the summertime. 'Erg', which has the same meaning, is a Celtic loan word 'airidh'. It would have found its way into Norse vocabulary during their occupation of Ireland, before their migration to Cumbria.

There are many second elements meaning 'a home'. 'Ham' which becomes Modern English 'home' was known in Old English as 'ham' and in Old Norse as 'heimr' and was used widely in place-names. 'Wic' is an early Latin loan word, and was used to mean a dairy farm and perhaps a camp on a Roman road. 'Tun', which was the same in Old Norse and Old English, develops into Modern English 'town', originally meant 'a fence', then 'enclosure round a house', then 'homestead', then 'village'; this element's oldest form occurs in Celtic as 'dun' meaning a fortified place, and is found in place-names throughout Europe. 'By' is Old Scandinavian, more often Danish than Norwegian for 'home', as is 'thorpe' meaning a village.

'Thwaite', from ON thveit, is the second element that most typifies the place-names of Cumbria. It means land cleared of trees, brushwood, and rocks to be used for growing crops or keeping animals. It was not enclosed by a wall or fence and not large enough to be called a field by modern standards.

Many mysteries remain. Pikeawassa, Lickle, Dollywaggon Pike, to name but a few, will for ever be open to speculation. In the text, early forms have been supplied where there is doubt as to the meaning of the place-name. Where no early forms exist an educated guess has been attempted.

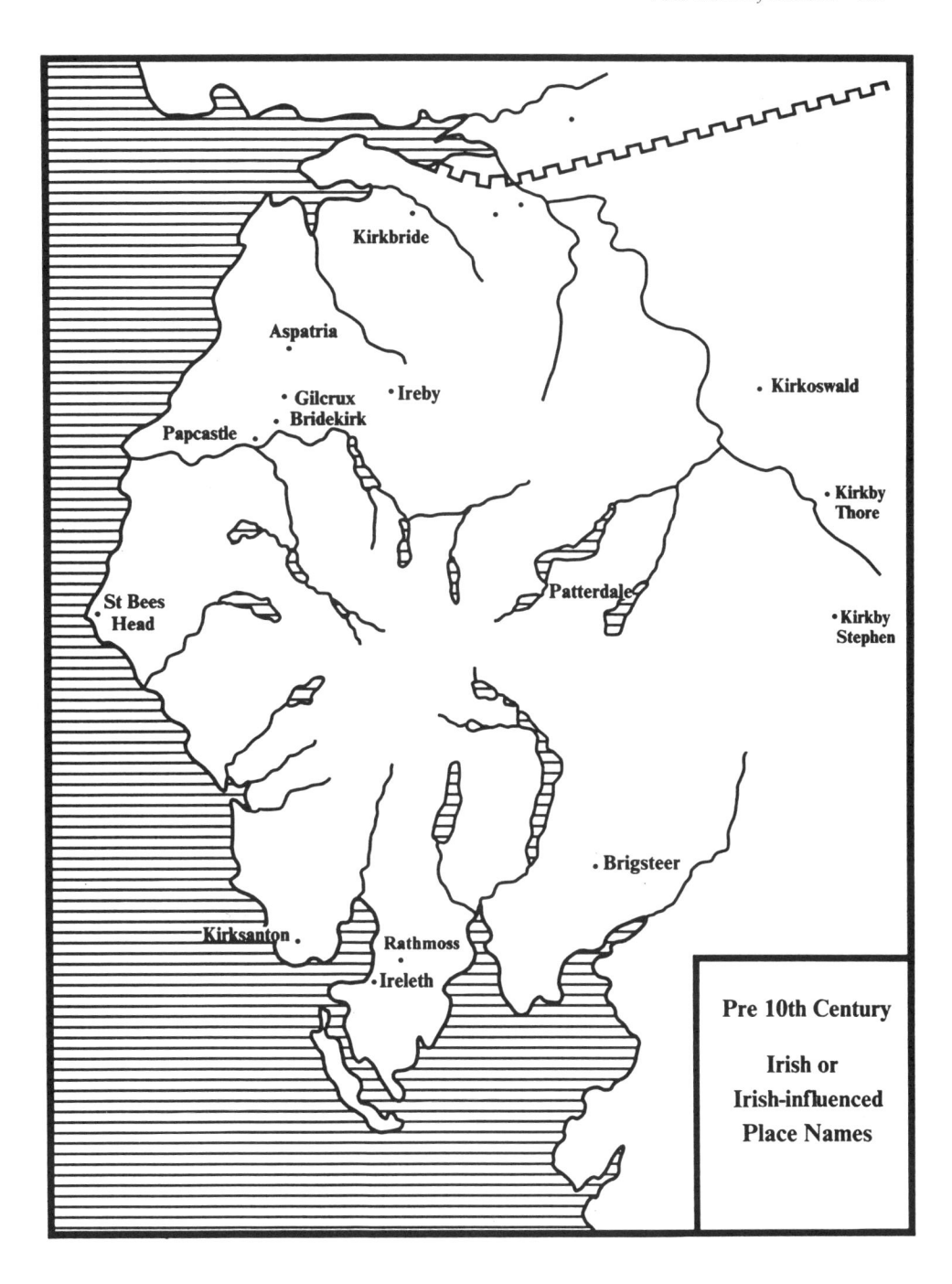

Place Names of Cumbria xix

Pre 10th Century

Irish or
Irish-influenced
Place Names

Abbreviations

EPNS	English Place Name Society.
Celtic	Brythonic Celtic spoken by the Britons of Cumbria.
OE	Old English. This was the language spoken by the Anglo-Saxons from the 6th to the 12th centuries. Anglian was the dialect in the north of England.
ON	Old Norse. This was the language spoken by Norwegians who colonised Iceland, Ireland, the Isle of Man, the Hebrides and north west England from the 9th to the 12th centuries.
ME	Middle English. This was the language spoken in England between the 12th and the 15th centuries. It was a development from Old English with influences of Scandinavian, Norman French and medieval Latin.
ð	This Runic character has been used in the text as a voiced and unvoiced fricative 'th', medially and finally.
*	Unrecorded form.

A

ACKENTHWAITE
Clearing amongst oak trees, from ON eik in the dative plural eikum, and ON thveit.

ADGARLEY
Eadgar's slope, the first element being an OE personal name, and the second element ON or OE hlið.

AGLIONBY
Argyllun's home, a Norman name, and Danish by.

AIKEN
At the oaks, from ON dative plural eikum.

AIKHEAD
Head (of valley, field) with an oak tree, from ON eik and ON hofuð 'head'.

AIKRIGG
Oak tree ridge, from ON eik and ON hryggr.

AIKSHAW
Oak wood, from ON eik and ON skogr.

AIKTON
Farm by an oak tree, from ON eik and ON tun.

AINSTABLE
An early form Ainstapelid 1178 shows this name to mean either fern covered hillside, from ON einstabi 'fern' and ON hlið, or one pillar of stone on a hillside, from ON einn, ON stopul and ON hlið. The latter explanation is feasible as there is evidence of early Celtic inhabitation in this region.

AIRA FORCE
Strong river, from Celtic Isara. Force is ON fors, 'waterfall'.

ALDINGHAM
Home of the descendants of Alda, from an OE personal name, OE inga 'descendants' and OE ham 'home'. This place-name was recorded with its present

spelling in Domesday Book. The remains of a Norman motte and bailey castle belonging to Michael le Fleming can be seen to the south-west of the village.

ALLERDALE
Valley of the river Ellen, from a Celtic name Alauna the meaning of which is unknown, and ON dalr.

ALLITHWAITE
Eilifr's clearing, the first element being a Norse personal name and the second from ON thveit 'clearing'.

ALLONBY
Aleyn's home. Aleyn is a Norman name and by is Danish.

ALSTON
Aldhun's farm, an OE personal name and OE tun 'farm'.

ALSTONBY
Home of Astin, which is a personal name found in the 13th century from Scandinavian Asketill. The second element is Danish by 'home'.

AMBLESIDE
Amal's summer hut or dairy farm, the second element being ON saetr. There are remains here at the head of Windermere of a Roman fort, named Galava.

ANGERTON
Hamlet on the bay from ON angr and ON tun. There are two places of this name, one situated on the estuary of the river Duddon, and the other on the channel of the River Wampool near Kirkbride, NE Cumbria.

ANGLE TARN
The early form Angilterne, 1266, would seem to show that the first element is ON ongull 'fishing hook', so the name could mean 'tarn where fishing took place'. There is a Norse word ongal meaning a bend, but as this tarn near Bowfell is almost completely circular, being in a corrie, it is unlikely that the name is based on this element. There is another tarn of this name east of Patterdale.

ANNASIDE
Summer hut of Einarr, a popular Norse personal name. The second element is ON saetr.

ANTHORN
A single thorn tree, from ON einn and ON thorn. East of the village and west

over the bridge there is a solitary thorn tree, near which (or near its predecessor) it was the custom to hold the local court.

APPLEBY
Dwelling by an apple tree, from either ON apaldr or OE aeppel and ON byr. Its earliest written form is Aplebi in 1130.

APPLEGARTH
Apple tree enclosure, from ON apaldr and ON garðr.

APPLETHWAITE
A clearing where apples grew, from ON epli, plural of apaldr, and ON thveit.

ARKLEBY
Home of Arkil, probably a Danish name as the second element is Danish by 'home'.

ARLECDON
Land in a valley cleared by burning, from Celtic ar 'on, in', llosg 'burnt ground', and OE denu 'valley'. Another proposed explanation of this name is 'valley of a stream frequented by eagles' from OE earn lacu denu.

ARMATHWAITE
The clearing of the hermit, from the early form Ermitethwayt 1232. There are three places of this name in Cumbria, and the one near Ainstable was the site of a nunnery founded by William Rufus.

ARMBOTH
Probably hermit's hut, from ME armite and ON buð. The first element could be a personal name such as Arni. An early form Armabothe 1530 is too late for positive identification. There are signposts to this place on the west shore of Thirlmere but there is nothing there now except foundations of a ruined house.

ARNABY
Ornulf's house, probably a Danish name here as the second element is Danish by 'home'.

ARNSIDE
An early form Arnuluesheved 1208 shows this name to mean Earnwulf's headland, from an OE personal name and OE heafod. Later forms Ernesyde 1537 and Arnesyd 1535 show how this place-name has changed.

ARRAD FOOT
No early forms but Arrad is possibly 'on the hill' from Celtic ar 'on' and Celtic ardd 'hill'. OE fota 'foot' would have been added later.

ARTHURET
There is no satisfactory explanation of this name. It was recorded in Welsh literature as Ardderyd and Armterid as the site of a battle which the Celtic Christians won. The first element could be Celtic ar 'on the', or ard 'hill' but the second element is obscure.

ARTHUR'S SEAT
Probably Celtic ar 'on the' and torr 'hill', compare Old Welsh twrr 'bulge', Gaelic torr 'hill' 'heap' and Cornish tor. There are other places which contain this name, such as Stone Arthur, and Arthuret (see above). Unfortunately it probably has nothing to do with the British king Arthur, who brilliantly defended the Celts against the advancing Saxons in the 6th century, although some of the medieval romances connected with Arthur are thought to be set in Cumbria. The second word, seat, is ON saetr 'shieling'.

ARTLEGARTH
Arnkell's enclosure, from an ON personal name and ON garðr.

ASBY
Ashi's home, probably Danish as the second element is by 'home'.

ASHLACK
Valley with ash trees, the second element being ON slakki, the first OE aesc.

ASHNESS
Headland with ash trees, from OE aesc and OE ness.

ASKERTON
Either Asgeirr's farm, or farm by an ash tree, from ON askr and ON tun.

ASKHAM
Either at the ash trees, from ON dative plural askum, or home by an ash tree, from ON askr and ON ham. There are several places with this name. Askam-in-Furness is spelt without the 'h'.

ASPATRIA
Patrick's ash tree, from ON askr and Irish personal name Patric. This is an example of an inversion compound, where the defining element comes last. Compare Brigsteer and Kirkoswald.

AUGHERTREE
An early form Alcotewraye 1540 shows this name to mean corner with an old cottage, from OE (e)ald cot meaning 'old cottage' and ON vra 'corner'. There are remains of a British settlement on the fell of this name north of Skiddaw.

AUSTHWAITE
Eastern clearing, from ON austr 'east' and ON thveit.

AYSIDE
Either hut by a river, from ON a 'river' and ON saetr, or hut by an oak tree, from ON eik and ON saetr.

B

BACKBARROW
Hill with a ridge, from OE baec and OE beorg. This name suits the topography near the village.

BAGGARAH
Either hawker's landmark, from ME bagger 'hawker', and ON ra 'landmark', or Baggi's corner, the second element being ON vra 'corner'. However in the Isle of Man the word baregarrow means rough land.

BAGGROW
As above. Both places are on old Roman roads.

BAMPTON
The early form Bamton, 1201, seems to show the meaning to be beam farm or farm made with a beam of wood, from OE beam and OE tun. The 'p' is intrusive and not part of the etymology.

BAND
The Band on Bow Fell means a projecting ridge, from ON bandr. Band is also a local dialect word meaning boundary.

BANDRAKE HEAD
A long narrow mountain, from ON bandr, with a sheepdroving road, from ON rak.

BANNISDALE
Valley of Banni, an Old Norse nickname for one who curses.

BANNISIDE
Either shieling of Banni, or Bennen, the second element being ON saetr.

BARBON
The village takes its name from the stream Barbon Beck meaning wild boar stream, from OE bar and OE brunne. It is possible the first element is OE bere 'corn', so the name then would mean stream running through a corn field. The ON bekkr 'stream' would have been added later.

BARDSEA
The earliest forms Berretseige in Domesday Book, and Berdeseia 1155, could refer to Celtic bard 'poet', 'minstrel', and eisteddfa 'seat' or 'resting place'. The second element could be ON ey 'island' or 'isolated hill rising out of flat land'. Bardsey Island off the coast of Wales was a place of mystery and pilgrimage. There is a stone circle called the druid circle on Birkrigg and many other indications of British settlement in the area which could have made this Bardsea have the same significance. However, other place-name researchers have suggested that the first element of this name is a personal name such as Beornred.

BARF
Hill from OE beorg.

BARNSCAR
The earliest forms of this name are Barnsea, 1774, and Barnscar and Bardskow on maps of 1794 which are rather late for positive identification. It would appear though that the name is a contracted form of borrans haugr which means a hill with ancient remains from OE borgaesn and ON haugr. There are remains of a prehistoric settlement here with many cairns and tumuli. Bronze Age burial urns have been found here.

BARROW-IN-FURNESS
Early forms Barrai 1190 and Barray 1292 seem to indicate 'headland island' from Celtic barr and ON ey. The Barra in the Outer Hebrides will have the same meaning, and is in a similar position, that is an island at the end of a body of land. The mountain Barrow, in Newlands, means hill, from OE beorg.

BARTON
Corn farm, from OE beretun.

BASSENTHWAITE
Bastun's clearing, from a Norman personal name and ON thveit.

A single thorn tree, as in the place-name Anthorn.

BAUGH
Possibly shoulder from ON bogr, or bow-shaped from ON bogi. Either explanation would suit this large fell east of Sedbergh.

BAYCLIFFE
The early form Belleclive 1212 seems to show French bel 'beautiful' and OE clif. There is an OE word bel 'signal fire' or 'funeral pyre' which could be the first element, referring either to a beacon or a cremation place.

BEACON
Many beacon hills exist in Cumbria which were used for ancient signalling purposes. The word comes from OE beacn.

BECKERMET
Meeting of streams, from ON bekkjar and ON mot. This village near Seascale is at the junction of two streams. Another possibility for the meaning of this name is hermit's stream from early forms such as Beckermeth 1291.

BEETHAM
Home on the river Bela, the original name of which was Beetha 'flat smooth river', from ON bioðr and ON a. The second element is ON heimr or OE ham. Bioðr actually meant 'table' but when referring to the land, meant 'flat'. In Domesday Book the place is called Biedun.

BELLE ISLE
Formerly Langholme 'long island' in Windermere, it was renamed after its purchase by Isabella Curwen in 1781.

BENN
Hill, from Gaelic beinn.

BERRIER
Hill shieling, from ON berg and ON erg.

BETHECAR
Gaelic personal name, Beathog's shieling, the second element being ON erg.

BEWALDETH
The earliest form, Bualdith 1255, shows the name to be an inversion compound, meaning the homestead of Aldgyth, from ON bu or byr and an ON feminine personal name.

BEWCASTLE
An old Roman fort belonging to Bueth. The first element could be ON buð or ON bu 'dwelling place', as above.

BIGGAR
Hut on a pasture where barley grows, from ON bygg 'barley' and ON erg.

BIGGARDS
Enclosures where barley grows. There are no early forms but it seems likely that the first element is ON bygg and the second element is ON garðr 'enclosure'.

BIGLANDS
Land where barley grows, from ON bygg 'barley' and ON land.

BIGRIGG
Ridge where barley grows, the second element being ON hryggr 'ridge'.

BIRBECK
Stream with birch trees, from ON birkr and ON bekkr.

BIRDOSWALD
Early forms Borddosewald circa 1200, Burthoswald, show this place to mean 'Oswald's fold' from an OE personal name and Celtic buarth. It is an Irish inversion compound where the defining element appears second.

BIRKBY
Home of the Britons, as shown by the early form Bretaby 1163. There are many remains of early settlements, cairns and burial mounds on this moor to the east of Ravenglass.

BIRKER
Birch hill, from ON birkr and ON haugr. The second element could be ON erg, in which case it means a birch shieling.

BIRKRIGG
Ridge where birch trees grow, from ON birkr and ON hryggr.

BIRKWRAY
Corner where birch trees grow, from ON birkr and ON vra 'corner'.

BLACK COMBE
This mountain near Millom has a pronounced black cwm or corrie to the east of the summit from which the name is derived. Celtic cwm becomes OE cumb.

There are other names using combe or coombe with a colour such as Green Coombe, White Coombe. It is possible the second element is OE camb 'ridge'.

BLACK SAIL
Black hollow, the second element being ON seila.

BLACKWELL
Either black well, from OE blaec and OE wella, or pale barren fields, from ON bleikr and ON vellir.

BLAGILL
Dark ravine, from ON bla and ON gil.

BLAITHWAITE
Pale clearing or Bleikr's clearing. Bleikr is ON for pale, or bleak.

BLAWITH
Dark wood, from ON bla and ON viðr.

BLEA BECK
Dark or blue stream, from ON bla and ON bekkr.

BLEA TARN
Dark or blue small lake, from ON bla and ON tjorn.

BLEA WATH
Dark wood. There are no early forms but as this place is not near a stream, it is unlikely that the second element is ON vaðr 'ford' as opposed to ON viðr 'wood'. The first element is from ON bla.

BLENCARN
Hill with a cairn, from Celtic blaen and carn.

BLENCATHRA
Possibly 'mountain of the stone circular fort', from the Celtic blaen and the genitive singular of cathair, cathrach, referring to the nearby Neolithic stone circle of Castlerigg. However, as Cathair can also mean a chair or seat (compare Cader Idris in Wales) Blencathra could mean the same as its modern English name, Saddleback, accurately describing its shape.

BLENCOGO
Possibly cuckoo's hill, from Celtic blaen 'hill', Celtic cog 'cuckoo' and ON haugr 'hill'.

BLENCOW
Hill top, from Celtic blaen 'hill', and ON haugr 'hill'.

BLENG
As this element, Celtic blaen, has several meanings such as 'end, edge, source of river, stream, highland', it can be found as the name of a river and a hill.

BLENNERHASSET
Hay pasture on a hill farm. Early forms Blendrerseta, Blennerheiseta, 1188, Blenhersete, 1190, and Blenerheyset,1235, seem to show a four syllabled hybrid form. The first two are Celtic blaen 'hill', and possibly dre 'farm', added to which are Norse heysaetr 'hay pasture'. There was a Roman fort here but that has not influenced the present name.

BLINDBOTHEL
Dwelling on a hill, from Celtic blaen 'hilltop' and ON bothl.

BLINDCRAKE
Top crag, from Celtic blaen 'hilltop' and Celtic carrec 'rock'.

BOLTON
Dwelling to which a farm has been added, from ON boðl, and ON tun.

BOONWOOD
Wood given on request, from ON bon 'plea'.

BOOT
Hut or outhouse, from ON buð. Another explanation could be 'bend', and as this hamlet is near the joining of the rivers Whillan and Esk this may well be correct.

BOOTH HOLME
Shed on a spit of land or island, from ON buð and ON holmr.

BOOTLE
Dwelling, from OE botl.

BORRANS
Burial mound, or any ancient pile of stones, from OE burgaesn. This word occurs quite frequently in Cumbria and also appears as Borwen and Burwain.

BORROWDALE
Valley of the fortified place, from ON borgar, genitive singular of borg and ON

dalr. There are two valleys of this name. The one south of Keswick refers to Castle Crag, a British hill fort, and the one north east of Kendal refers to the Roman fort at Low Borrow Bridge.

BORWICK
Corn farm, from OE bere and OE wic.

BOTCHERBY
Bochard's home, a French form of Germanic Burchard. The second element is Danish by 'home'.

BOTCHERGATE
As above but the second element is ON gata 'road'.

BOTHEL
Dwelling, from ON boðl.

BOUTH
Dwelling place, from ON buð. However, an early form Bowith, 1287, suggests curved wood from ON bogi and ON viðr. Bowith was also mentioned in the Court Rolls of Henry VIII.

BOWDERDALE
Valley with huts, from ON buðar and ON dalr, or boulder-strewn valley with the first element dialectic bowder as below.

BOWDER STONE
Bowder is a dialectal form of boulder.

BOW FELL
An early form, Bowesfel 1242 seems to indicate that the first element is a personal name rather than ON bogi 'curved, bow shaped'. The name Bowe appears in 1333 on a Cumberland deed.

BOWLAND
Either Bolli's land, or farmstead with land, from ON buð and ON land, or curved land, from ON bogi 'bow'.

BOWNESS-ON-SOLWAY
Curved promontory, from ON bogi and ON nes. There is another Bowness of the same meaning on Bassenthwaite Lake.

BOWNESS-ON-WINDERMERE
Bull's headland. An early form, Bulnes, 1282, suggests that the first element is from OE bula 'bull', and the second element is OE ness 'headland'.

BOWSCALE
Bolli's hut, or bow-shaped hut, from ON bogi and ON skali.

BRACELET
Second element means a flat piece of land, from ON slettr. The first part could be 'broad', from ON breiðr, but the earliest recordings are 17th century, which is too late to give clues.

BRACKENSLACK
Valley with bracken, from Old Scandinavian brakni and ON slakkr 'valley'. Bracken could be a personal name.

BRACKENTHWAITE
Clearing with bracken, from Old Scandinavian brakni and ON thveit.

BRAITHWAITE
Broad clearing, from ON breiðr and ON thveit.

BRAMPTON
Hamlet by the post, from ON brandr and ON tun, or Brandr's hamlet. The meaning could also be 'farm where broom grew', from OE brom and OE ton, or 'farm where there were brambles', from ME brame.

BRANDRETH
There are two fells of this name, one north of Great Gable, and the other west of Thirlmere. This second one is actually named Threefooted Brandreth and was the point where three ancient boundaries met. A brandreth is a dialectal word meaning grid-iron or trivet, from ON brandreið 'grate'. A beacon could have been lit in such a receptacle.

BRANSTY
Steep path, from OE brant and OE stig.

BRANTHWAITE
An early form Bromthweit 1210 suggests either broom clearing or bramble clearing. There is a ME word brame 'bramble' so there probably was a similar word in ON.

BRANTWOOD
Burnt wood, from OE brent and OE wudu.

BRATHAY
Broad river, from ON breiðr and ON a.

BRATS HILL
There are no early forms of this name. Because of the burial mounds found on this moor between Wasdale and Eskdale, showing early occupation, the name could be a corruption of ON Breta, 'of the Britons'.

BRAYSTONES
Broad stones, from OE brad or ON breiðr and OE stan, or ON steinn.

BRAYTON
Broad hamlet, from ON breiðr and ON tun.

BRETARGH HOLT
Summer pasture of the Britons, from ON Breta and ON ergh. OE holt 'wood' was added later.

BRETHERDALE
Brothers' valley, from ON broeðir and ON dalr. The first element here is used in the genitive plural broeðra.

BRIGHAM
Home by the bridge, from ON bryggia or OE brycg and OE ham.

BRIGSTEER
Styr's bridge, from an ON personal name and ON bryggia. This is an Irish influenced inversion compound, where the defining element comes second instead of first. There is no bridge here now, but on the level valley floor below the village, there is evidence of draining, containing and possibly rerouting the River Pool, which in bygone times could have flowed closer to the hillside.

BRISCOE
Birch wood, from ON birkr and ON skogr. This could also be ON bretaskogi which would then mean 'wood of the Britons'.

BROCKLEBANK
Bank where there are badgers' sets, from OE brocc-hol and ME banke (from Old Danish banke).

BROTHERILKELD
From early forms such as Butherulkul 1210, this name means Ulfkell's huts,

from an OE personal name and ON buða, plural of buð 'hut'. This is an example of an inversion compound showing Irish influence.

BROTHERSWATER
Brother's lake, from ON broðir and ON vatn. There is a local tale that this lake was named after two brothers who drowned in a skating accident. However, some early forms suggest that the first element is 'broad', from ON breiðr.

BROUGH
Fort, from OE burg. Brough in Stainmore was on the Roman road that ran from York to Penrith. There are several places of this name.

BROUGHAM
Roman Brocavum. There is much evidence of earlier fortifications in this area at the junction of the rivers Eamont and Eden. The Romans built a fort here to defend the major crossroads of the north-south and east-west trunk routes. It has been suggested that the local British word for badger, 'broch', could have been borrowed by the Romans, so Brocavum could mean 'place where badgers live'. Brougham could also mean 'homestead by the fort', from OE burh and OE ham.

BROUGHTON
Farm on a brook, from OE broc and OE tun. There are several places of this name.

BROWNBER
Brown hill, from OE brun and OE beorg.

BROWNRIGG
Ridge on the edge of a declivity, from ON brun 'cliff' and ON hryggr. The first element could be an ON personal name Brunr.

BRUNSTOCK
The early form Bruneskayth 1253 shows the second element to be ON skeið 'racecourse'. The first element may be ON bruni 'land cleared by burning', or ON brunnr 'well or spring'.

BURGH BY SANDS
A Roman fort near the Solway Firth, from either OE burg or ON borg 'fortified place'.

BURNESIDE
An early form Brunolvesheved 1235 shows the name to mean Brunwulf or Brunolf's headland. The second element is from OE heafod 'headland'.

BURNMOOR
The moor of borrans or ancient remains, from OE borgaesn and OE mor. There are several stone circles and cairns on this tract of land, and an ancient enclosure known as Maiden Castle near Burnmoor Tarn.

BURRELS
Grave, from OE byrgels. There are several hills and mounds of this name, occasionally spelt Birrels. The word was mistaken for a plural form in the Middle Ages and the 's' was dropped. The modern English word is burial.

BURROW
Hill from OE beorg.

BURTON
Fortified farm, or farm of the fortified place, from OE burg and OE tun.

BUSTABECK
Farmhouse by a stream, from ON bustaðr and ON bekkr.

BUTHERHALS
Narrow neck of land between huts, from ON buðar and ON hals 'neck'.

BUTTERMERE
Huts by the lake, from ON buðar and OE mere. There is a possibility the meaning could be 'lake where butter was made', from OE butere. It is mentioned in Domesday Book as Butremere.

BUTTERWICK
Possibly butter-making farm, from OE butere and OE wic, c.f. Keswick.

C

CAERMOTE
This is the name of a small but prominent hill immediately behind a Roman fort a mile north of Bassenthwaite Lake. The etymology is obscure though the first element is Celtic caer 'fortified'. The second element could be OE gemot 'meeting place', as in Moota Hill.

Place Names of Cumbria 17

Brotherswater: possibly named after two brothers drowned here in a skating accident.

Caldbeck in c.1910, showing the 'cold stream' which gives the village its name.

CALDBECK
Cold stream, from ON kald and ON bekkr.

CALDER
A British river name meaning violent or rapid water, from Celtic caled and dubro.

CALDEW
Cold water, from Old Anglian cald and OE ea.

CALGARTH
Enclosure for calves, from ON kalfar and ON garðr.

CALTHWAITE
Either clearing for calves, or Karli's clearing.

CALVA
Calf hill, from ON kalfr and ON haugr. This could have been a hill on which calves were kept, or it could refer to a small hill next to a bigger one.

CAM SPOUT
Waterfall from a ridge, from OE camb 'ridge' and ME spoute 'a gushing jet' of water.

CAPPLEBARROW
No early forms but probably 'horse hill' from ON kapall and ON berg.

CARDALE
Valley with a fort, from British caer and ON dalr. There is evidence of defensive structures in the Eamont valley from pre-Roman times.

CARDUNNETH PIKE
Fort of Dinoot, a British personal name. The first element is British caer 'fort'.

CARDURNOCK
Fort on a pebbly place, from British caer 'fort' and Gaelic dornach. It is situated on the coast.

CARGO
Rocky hill, from Old Welsh carrec and ON haugr.

CARK
Stone or rock, from Old Welsh carrec.

CARLES
This is the name of the Castlerigg stone circle near Keswick. It is originally from Latin corolla 'garland, circle, coronet', the earliest sense of the word being 'ring, circle or ring dance'. Stonehenge was known as the Carol. The word probably entered the English language through Old French carole, after the Norman Conquest. It is possible that this is the first element in names such as Carleton, Carlatton.

CARLETON
There are several places of this name, all near where stone circles are known to have stood. It is possible that the first element could be carol as above under Carles, though it is generally thought to be ON karli 'free peasant'. The second element is OE or ON tun 'farm'.

CARLINGWHA
Kerling's hill, or old hag's hill, as ON kerling means an old woman. The second element is ON haugr.

CARLISLE
The fortified city of Luguvallium which becomes Luwel in primitive Welsh (6th to the 8th century). This becomes Luel and evolves into modern Lisle. Old Welsh cair (modern Welsh caer) 'fortified city' had been prefixed by the 9th century. Luguvallium, a Romano-British name, could mean the wall of the Celtic god Lug, or strong as the god Lug. Lug appears as first element in several place names in areas occupied by Celts, such as Lugudunum which develops into modern Lyons, France.

CARLTON
Karli's farm or free peasant's farm, from ON karli and ON tun. See also Carleton above.

CARR HOLM
Island or water meadow in a swamp, from ON kjarr and ON holmr. The first element could be 'rock' from Old Welsh carrec.

CARTMEL
A British name, as Camden, the 16th century historian, says that Cartmel and all the Britons with it were given to St Cuthbert in the year 677 AD. The most probable elements are Celtic carrec 'rock' and Celtic moel 'hill'. The fell east of the village, Hampsfield Fell, is an unusually stony limestone outcrop. The name Cartmel was transferred to the village when it developed. Other place-name researchers, notably Eilert Ekwall, propose the meaning 'sand bank in rocky

ground' from ON kartr melr, but there is no sand here, and the name was recorded a good 200 years before the Norse arrived in Cumbria.

CARTMEL FELL
A hillside 7 miles north of Cartmel, probably farmed by Cartmel Priory. The parish of Cartmel extends to Staveley-in-Cartmel to the west and Cartmel Fold to the north.

CASTERTON
Farm by the Roman fort. This place is situated on a Roman road. The first element is OE caester, a Latin loan-word from castra 'camp', and the second OE tun.

CASTLE CARROCK
A stone castle or castle on a rock, from Celtic castell, a loan word from Latin castellum, and Celtic carrec 'rock' or 'stone'. Probably all the names with castle like Castle Head and Castle How were fortified places of refuge for the Britons.

CAT BELLS
Wild cat hills, from Celtic kat and moel. In Celtic B and M are often interchanged. Moel meaning 'hill' has become bell. An alternative explanation is that bell is from ON belja 'bell shaped'.

CAT BIELDS
This fell north of Wastwater means 'wild cats' shelters', from Celtic kat or ON kati and a Scottish and northern English dialect word bield.

CATSTYCAM
The name probably means wild cat's path on a ridge, from ON katr, ON stigr and OE camb.

CAUDALE
No early forms. The name could mean cold valley, from ON kaldr and ON dalr, or calf valley, from ON kalfr.

CAUSEY PIKE
Causeway or embankment, from Celtic cawsai. This explanation fits the shape of the mountain.

CAW
Calf, meaning a small hill next to a larger one, an amalgamation of ON kalfr and ON haugr.

CAWDALE
Probably calf valley, from ON kalfr and ON dalr.

CLAIFE
Ridge of cliffs, from ON kleif. This is still visible at the top of Claife Heights near Hawkshead.

CLAPPERSGATE
Path with stepping stones over a river. The second element is ON gata 'path', and the first element is a dialectal word clopper 'natural bridge'.

CLAWTHORPE
Clerk's village, as is shown by an early form Clerkethorpe 1277. In the 13th century, a clerk would be an ordained minister of the church, or a learned man. Thorpe is an Old Danish word.

CLEATOR
Shieling by the cliffs or rocks, from ON klettr and ON erg.

CLIFBURN
Spring by the cliff, from ON klif and ON brunnr.

CLIFTON
Hamlet by the cliff, from ON klif and ON tun.

CLOFFOCKS
Hill with clefts or ravines, from ON klauf 'cleft' and ON haugr 'hill'.

CLOUGH
Cleft or ravine, from ON klauf. This word has survived in the dialect of North Lancashire.

COCKEN
This was a village near Ormsgill in Barrow, now lost, on land reclaimed in 14th century Furness by the monks of Furness Abbey for agricultural purposes. Apparently they named it Cockaigne after the mythical never-never land. However, the meaning could be hillock from Celtic cocyn. There are no early forms before the 14th century.

COCKERMOUTH
Mouth of the river Cocker, a British river name, from kukro, meaning crooked.

COCKLEY
Sparse wood with wild birds, from OE cocc and OE leah.

COCKUP
No early forms but the name probably means bird valley from OE cocc and OE hop. Although this is the name of several fells near Skiddaw, Great Cockup, Little Cockup and Cockup, the name probably derived from the deep valley between them through which runs the Cumbrian Way.

COLBY
Koli's home, the second element being Danish by, the first a Danish personal name.

COLEDALE
No early forms. It could be Koli's valley but there was a Celtic word coll 'hazel' so the meaning could be valley where hazels grew. It is also possible that the name means charcoal valley, from ON kol and ON dalr.

COLTON
Probably farm where colts were raised, from OE colt and OE tun.

COLWITH
Charcoal burners' wood, from ON kola 'charcoal burner' and ON viðr 'wood'.

CONGRA MOSS
Congar is a Welsh saint's name. Moss means boggy or mossy ground from OE mos or ON mosi.

CONISHEAD
King's head, from ON konungr and ON hofuð. The Priory was founded by Augustinians in the reign of Henry II as a hospital. It also provided shelter for those who crossed the sands of Morecambe Bay.

CONISTON
An early form Coningeston 1157 shows this name to mean king's hamlet or manor. It may be an adaptation from OE cyningestun, but it is more probably Scandinavian. ON konungr could also be a personal name.

CONISTON WATER
This was originally named Thorsteinn's lake.

COPELAND
Land which has been bought, from ON kaupland.

CORNEY
Possibly heron island, from OE *corn, *cron, a side form of OE cran 'heron' and OE eg 'island'.

COTEHILL
Cottage on a hill, from OE cot 'cottage', 'shelter for animals' and OE hyll.

COWAN
Cow house, from OE cu-aern.

CRABSTACK
Krabbi's heap or pile, from ON stakkr and an ON personal name.

CRACKENTHORPE
Kraka's village. Kraka could be a nickname for one who walks with difficulty. Thorpe is Old Danish.

CRAKE
An opening formed in the sand marshes by the tide, or creek, from ON kreik. The name could be 'rocky stream' from Old Welsh creic.

CRINKLE CRAGS
Either rocks that surround, from ON kringla 'ring', or Grimkell's crags. It is also possible that it means 'wrinkled', from an OE word cringol. The last explanation seems the most likely, as the crags are gnarled looking.

CROGLIN
An early form, Crokelyn 1140, suggests crooked lake or stream, from ON krokr and Celtic llyn. The first element could be Celtic cruc 'hill', so the name would mean stream by the hill. There is no lake here now.

CROOK
There are two possible explanations of the name of this village west of Kendal. The first is 'bend' from ON krokr, but the beck that runs through the village has no conspicuous bend. The second explanation, 'hill' from Celtic cruc suits the topography much better. There is another Crook meaning 'hill' north east of Sedbergh.

CROOKEDHOLM
Bent island or water meadow, from ON krokr and ON holmr.

CROOKLANDS
Land in the bend in the river, or in the fork where two rivers meet, from ON krokr and OE or ON land.

CROSBY
Hamlet by the cross (probably not religious, more a landmark or guide post), from ON kross and ON byr.

CROSBY GARRET
As above. The French personal name Gerard would have been added in Norman times.

CROSBY RAVENSWORTH
As above. The affix is an ON personal name Hrafnsvartr.

CROSSCANONBY
Originally Crosseby Canoun 1285. This was a part of Crosby in Allerdale given to the canons of Carlisle.

CROSSCRAKE
Kraki's cross, from a Norse personal name and ON kross.

CROSSDALE
Valley with a cross, from ON kross and ON dalr.

CROSTHWAITE
Clearing with a cross, from ON kross and ON thveit. St. Kentigern established a church here, near Keswick.

CRUMMOCK WATER
An early form Crombocwater 1308 shows the first element to be British crumbo with the diminutive oc (see Penruddock) meaning 'little crooked one'. OE waeter would have been added later.

CULGAITH
Either retreat wood, from Celtic cilgoed, where a monk or hermit would have had his 'cell', or narrow wood from Celtic culgoed.

CUMBERLAND
The land of the Cumbrians or Britons from Welsh Cymri, from an Old Celtic root kombrogi 'fellow countrymen'. This county name was first used in 1177 after the region was recaptured from the Scots in 1157.

CUMBRIA
In 875 AD the kingdom of the Cumbri is referred to, whose name was Cymru, translated into Medieval Latin as Cumbria. For over a century, Cumbria, Strathclyde, and other old kingdoms were in a confederation known as Alba. In 1092,

William Rufus defeated Dunmail (Domhnuil), the last Celtic king of Cumbria and annexed it to England. The region was captured by the Scots in the reign of Stephen, and on its recovery in 1157, during the reign of Henry II, Cumbria was divided into the counties of Cumberland, Westmorland and North Lancashire. They were reunited as Cumbria in 1974.

CUMDIVOCK
Valley of the little black one, referring to a stream, from Celtic cwm 'valley' and dyfoc 'little black one'.

CUMMERSDALE
The valley of the Cymri.

CUMREW
Valley by the hill-side, from Old Welsh cwm and rhiw. The name could also mean hillside of the Britons, the first element then being Cymri.

CUMWHITTON
An old Cumbrian name meaning valley, from Old Welsh cwm, of Whittington, which itself means 'farm of Hwita's descendants'.

CUNNINGARTH
Rabbit warren, from ME cuning erthe. There was an Anglo-Norman word coning which became modern English cony 'rabbit'. Erthe is from OE eorthe.

CUNSEY
Possibly river where there were rabbits, from Old French conys, plural of conil 'rabbit' and OE ea. Cunsey Beck runs from Esthwaite Water to Windermere. There is a possibility that the first element could be OE cyninges 'of the king'.

CURTHWAITE
A church in a clearing, from ON kirkja and ON thveit.

D

DACRE
Dacore was a British river name, meaning trickling stream. Compare Welsh deigr. The hamlet of Dacre is named after the river on which it stands. It seems likely that this is the Dacre mentioned by Bede in the 7th century where a monastery was being built in his time. In the graveyard of the church carved and plain stones laid in a pattern were found during the 1920s, which seem to be a primitive

sewage channel for a large building. The charming old church of St. Andrew houses the remains of two Celtic crosses, intricately carved.

DALEMAIN
Mani's valley. This is an inversion compound, like Aspatria 'Patrick's ash tree'. It is possible that the second element is stone from Celtic maen, so the meaning would be standing stone in a valley. There is a Celtic fort nearby.

DALSTON
Dali's hamlet, a personal name with OE or ON tun.

DALTON
Hamlet in a valley, from ON dalr and ON tun. There are several places of this name.

DEARHAM
Enclosure for deer, from OE deor and OE hamm.

DEE
This is a British river name meaning 'water', from Celtic dubro, which is derived from Latin deva meaning goddess. This would suggest that the River Dee was holy to the Britons.

DENDRON
Clearing in a valley, from OE denu and OE rum.

DENT
Valley of the river Dee, from Dee and Celtic nant 'valley'. Compare Derwent below.

DENTON
Farm in a valley, from OE denu and OE tun.

DERWENT
A British river name, meaning river where oaks grow, from Celtic derw 'oak tree' and nant 'valley, glen, ravine, brook'. Oak groves were sacred to the British. Borrowdale Valley, through which the Derwent flows, is still thickly wooded with oak trees.

DEVOKE WATER
A British word dyfoc, meaning the little black one. The tarn is small and of dark appearance.

Otterbield Bay, Derwent Water

DISTINGTON
Probably home of the descendants of a person with a name like Dyrst. Ington and Ingham are common OE place-name elements meaning 'home of the descendants of'.

DOCKER
Docca's shieling, or shieling in a valley, from ON dokkr 'valley' and ON erg 'shieling'.

DOCKWRAY
Corner in a valley, from ON dokkr and ON vra 'corner'.

DOCTOR'S BRIDGE
Doctor Edward Tyson, in 1734, had this bridge in Eskdale widened to allow his carriage to cross.

DODD
Round hill. The name is found in northern and Scottish dialects.

DOLLYWAGGON
No positive explanation for this name but perhaps a dollywaggon was a type of conveyance used to move ore down mountainsides. It is known that Elizabeth I imported 40 to 50 Germans to prospect for gold, silver, copper and quicksilver in Cumbria. They did work a copper mine above Thirlspot on Helvellyn.

DOLPHINHOLME
Probably a personal name Dolfin and ON holmr 'islet'.

DOVEDALE
No early forms but possibly dark valley, from British dubo- meaning black or dark, and ON dalr.

DOVENBY
Dufan's home. The Scandinavian personal name Dufan is a loan from Old Irish Duban and also means dark peak or beacon. The second element is ON byr or Old Danish by.

DOW CRAGS
Dark crags, from British dubo-, as above.

DRAGLEY
Dragon hill or tumulus, from OE draca and OE hlaw.

DRIGG
A place to drag a boat, a portage, from Old Scandinavian drag. Drigg is on the river Irt, which runs parallel with the sea for 2 miles, separated by a narrow stretch of land.

DRUMBURGH
Ridge near the fort, from Celtic drum 'ridge' and OE burg. The place is near Burgh by Sands on Hadrian's Wall.

DUDDON
This river name is of British origin with elements resembling modern Welsh dofn 'deep', and afon 'river'. The first element could also be Celtic dubo- 'dark', which was used quite frequently to describe water. The Norse settlers a thousand years later would have interpreted this name as Duðn. (See Dunnerdale).

DUFTON
The early form Dufton 1289 does not offer much help in assessing the meaning of this name. It could either mean 'dove farm', from ON dufa and ON tun or the first element could be a personal name as in Dovenby above.

DUNGEON GHYLL
A dark subterranian ravine, from ME donjon 'dungeon' and ON gil. This is a descriptive name for the waterfall which falls spectacularly down the slopes of the Langdale Pikes.

DUNMAIL RAISE
Cairn of stones of Dunmail, the last Celtic king of the Cumbri. The second element is ON hreysi. The story goes that Dunmail's crown fell off during the battle that took place here, and rolled into a bog from which it was never recovered. He was defeated by William Rufus leading an English army, who then annexed Cumbria to England.

DUNMALLET
This is the name of Celtic settlement on a small rounded hill near Pooley Bridge, Ullswater. Dun means 'fortified place' and mallet could be a personal name, or have some connection with Celtic moel 'hill'. Another explanation could be 'fort of curses', from Gaelic Dun Mallacht. This could be a reference to some slaughter which had taken place here.

DUNNERDALE
Valley of the river Duðn. Duðnar is the ON genitive singular of Duðn.

DUNNERHOLME
Island in the valley of the river Duddon. Holme is from ON holmr, and the first element shows the genitive singular of Duðn. (See Duddon above).

DURDAR
Oak copse, from Gaelic doire dorach.

E

EAMONT
Probably meeting of streams, from OE ea and OE gemot, here referring to the rivers Dacre and Eamont.

EASBY
Dwelling near ash trees, from ON eski which is the plural of ON askr 'ash tree', and ON byr.

EASEDALE
Valley of ash trees, from ON eski and ON dalr. The first element could also be OE eas, genitive singular of ea 'of the river', which is dominant in this valley near Grasmere.

ECCLERIGG
? Church on a ridge, from British ecles, from Latin ecclesia, and ON hryggr. It is possible that the first element is a personal name Eccel.

EDEN
British river name Ituna, meaning to gush forth. The broad and fertile valley of the river Eden was the corridor along which people travelled between the east of Northern England and the west via the Stainmore pass. A Roman road ran from York to Carlisle but there surely was a route there before then. Angles and Danes infiltrated Cumbria this way in the ensuing centuries. Apparently the Celtic language survived in the Eden Valley until the 14th century.

EEA
The river of this name runs through Cartmel and means simply river, from OE ea 'stream' or 'river'.

EEL CRAG
Steep crag, from ON illr. Illr generally meant bad or evil, but when applied to the topography probably meant 'difficult'.

EGREMONT
The barony of Copeland was granted by Henry I to William Meschines, who died in 1134. He built his motte at Egremont, calling the place a Norman name Aigremont.

EHEN
This is a British river name related to Welsh iain 'cold'.

ELLABARROW
Mound with alder trees, from ON elri and ON berg or OE beorg. (See Pennington).

ELLARIGG
Ridge with alder trees, from ON elri and ON hryggr.

ELLEN
This is a British river name Alaun of unknown meaning.

ELTERWATER
Swan lake, from ON eltr and ON vatn.

ELVA PLAIN
An early form Elfhow 1488 shows the second element to be ON haugr 'hill'. The first element could be an ON feminine personal name Elfr. There has been some speculation that the first element could refer to elves, as there is a stone circle nearby, which could have been regarded superstitiously.

ENNERDALE
Either Anund's valley, in the genitive singular Anundar and ON dalr, or valley of the Ehen, a British river name.

ESK
Either 'ash trees', from ON eski, or more likely a British river name Isca, compare Irish easc 'water', as in River Exe.

ESKDALE
Ash tree valley, or valley of Isca river.

ESKETT
Head of a valley with ash trees, from ON eski and ON hofuð. It is possible that it could be 'race course', from ON hestaskeið.

ESKHAUSE
Pass with ash trees, from ON eski and ON hals 'a neck of land, a pass'.

ESKMEALS
Sand dunes of the River Esk, the second element being ON melr 'sand dune'. The place is situated at the mouth of the River Esk.

ESPS
Aspen tree, from ON espi, a side form of osp.

ESPLAND HALL
Land with aspen trees.

ESTHWAITE
Early forms are lacking, but as there are several names with Ees around this small lake, such as Ees Wyke, Ees Hows and Strickland Ees, it would seem that the first element is OE eas 'of the water', genitive singular of OE ea. The name would then mean clearing by the lake, the second element being ON thveit.

EWEDALE
An early form, Ulvedale 1189, suggests wolf valley, or Ulfr's valley.

F

FAIRFIELD
Probably sheep hill, from ON faer 'sheep' and ON fjallr. There is a possibility that it could be beautiful hill from OE faeger and OE feld.

FARLETON
This place is mentioned in Domesday Book and probably means the farm of Faraldr, a Norse name. The same name is given to a nearby hill.

FELL
A mountain, from ON fjallr.

FENWICK
Farm on marshy land, from OE fenn and OE wic.

FINGLAND
Probably fair valley, from Celtic finn glenn. There is one early form Thingland 1279, which could suggest 'parliament field' from ON thing land, but the first explanation is more likely.

FINSTHWAITE
Clearing belonging to Finnr, from an ON personal name and ON thveit.

FLAKEBRIDGE
A crossing made of logs over a marsh, from ON flaki and OE brycg. Pathways like these, made in prehistoric times, are referred to as corduroy roads.

FLAKE HOW
Flak's hill, from an ON personal name and ON haugr. It is possible that the first element could be from ON flaki as above.

FLAN HILL
? Hill where there are sudden gusts of wind. There is an ON word flan meaning a sudden gust of wind.

FLASS
Swamp, from ME flasshe, originally from an ON word flask.

FLEET HOLME
Islet in a shallow channel, from ON fljot 'sheet of water' and ON holmr 'islet'.

FLEETWITH
The earliest form Fleetwath 1783 seems to show the name to mean ford over an inlet, from ON fljot 'inlet, sheet of water' and ON vaðr 'ford'. Perhaps Fleetwith Pike's name originated at the foot of the mountain showing a ford over Gatesgarthdale Beck which flows into Buttermere.

FLIMBY
An early form Flemingby 1174, shows this name to mean home of the Flemings. The second element is ON byr or Old Danish by.

FLIT HOLME
As Fleet Holme above.

FLOOKBOROUGH
Floki's hill, or fortified mound. The earliest record of this name is in 1246. A kind of fish, a fluke, from OE flōc, is caught in this area, but it seems more likely that the first element is a personal name. The second element is ON borg.

FLOSH
Pool or marshy place, from ME flosshe or flasshe.

FLUSCO
Possibly flat wood, from ON flatskogr, or wood in a marshy place with the first element as above.

FORCE MILL
Mill by a waterfall, from ON fors. This will be a comparatively late name, as water mills were unknown in Cumbria before the 13th century.

FOULNEY
Island of birds, from ON fugl in the genitive plural fuglena and ON ey.

FOULSHAW
Bird wood, from OE fugol and OE scaga.

FOXFIELD
Self explanatory.

FRIARS CRAG
Traditionally, this promontory on Derwentwater was where St. Cuthbert parted from St. Herbert when the latter became a hermit on the island of St. Herbert.

FRITH
Woodland, from OE fyrhth.

FRIZINTON
Home of the descendants of Fresa.

FROSWICK
Farm by a waterfall, from ON fors 'waterfall' and OE wic 'farm' from Latin vicus. This name refers to a cove on the Roman road which still runs up Troutbeck today. Blue Gill tumbles down the fellside here. The name is extended to the mountain behind.

FURNESS
Early form Fuðthernessa 1150, Fudernesium 1127, seems to show this name to mean further promontory, from OE furðra and OE ness. The old way to Furness was over the sands of Morecambe Bay. It began at Hest Bank, Lancashire, and progressed to Kent's Bank, the first promontory. The 'further promontory' was reached from Sandgate to Conishead.

G

GAISGILL
Ravine of the wild geese, from ON gas and ON gil. Gasgill has the same meaning.

GAMBLESBY
Home of Gamall, a Scandinavian personal name. The second element is Old Danish by.

GARRIGILL
Ravine or valley of Gerard, an Old French personal name of Germanic origin.

GARSDALE
Grass valley, from OE gaers and OE dael, or ON dalr.

GASCOW
Enclosed wood, from ON garðr 'fenced in area' and ON skogr.

GATESCALES
Huts belonging to Geiti, or goats' huts, from ON geiti 'goats' and ON skali 'huts'. The first element could be ON gata 'path'. The name would then mean huts on a path.

GATESGARTHDALE
Valley with a path through a gap, a mountain pass, from ON gata 'path', ON scarðr 'gap' and ON dalr 'valley'. This valley leads to Honister Pass from Buttermere. There is another Gatescarth Pass between Haweswater and Longsleddale.

GATESGILL
Early forms such as Gaytescales 1279, show this name to be the same as the one above.

GAWTHROP
Probably Gaukr's village, where the Old Danish thorpe shows metathesis of the 'r'.

GAWTHWAITE
Gaukr's clearing, from an ON personal name and ON thveit. Gaukr also means 'cuckoo' in ON, and an alternative meaning could be 'cuckoo's clearing'.

GILCRUX
The early forms Killcruce and Gillecruz, 1230, seem to show the first element is Irish cill, dative of cell 'church' and Celtic crug 'hill', so the name would mean 'at the church on the hill'.

GILDERDALE
Valley of traps, from ON gildri and ON dalr.

GILPIN
A river and bridge named after a well known family in the area.

GILSLAND
Possibly servant's land, from ON gilli, originally from Old Irish gilla. Another explanation could be the land of Gilles, a Celtic personal name meaning servant of Jesus.

GIMMER CRAG
No early forms but possibly sheep crag. Gimmer is a Cumbrian dialect word for sheep.

GLARAMARA
Shieling by the chasms, from ON gliufr in the dative gliufrum 'by the chasms' and ON erg. The first recording of this name, in the Coucher book of Furness Abbey shows 'Houedgleuermerhe', the first element being ON hofuð 'head', which is now lost.

GLASSON
Early form Glassan 1260 seems to show this name to mean small stream, from Old Irish glasan.

GLASSONBY
Glasson's home, from a possibly Irish personal name and Old Danish by.

GLEASTON
Farm on the river. Glas is a Celtic word for stream or river. A swift stream fed mainly from springs runs through this Furness village.

GLENCOYNE
Beautiful valley, from Celtic glenno 'valley' and Irish cain 'beautiful'. Compare modern Gaelic and Irish gleann and Welsh glyn.

GLENDHU
Dark valley, from British glennu and British dhu.

GLENRIDDING
Valley with bracken, from Celtic glenno 'valley' and Welsh rhedyn 'bracken'.

GOADSBARROW
There are no early forms but the meaning is probably the tumulus or burial mound of a person with the name of Godi or Gauti. The second element is from OE beorg.

Place Names of Cumbria 37

Signpost near Lowick Green: all the place-names are of Norse origin.

Gilsland Station, now closed, on the Newcastle-Carlisle railway.

GOLDSCOPE
This is a comparatively recent name, being a corruption of German Gottesgab 'the gift of God'. This was given by the Augsburg miners from 1566 to the vein of copper found in the Newlands Valley.

GOSFORTH
Goose ford, from OE gos and OE ford.

GOWBARROW
Windy hill, from ON gol 'gust of wind' and ON berg, or OE beorg.

GOWK
Cuckoo from ON gaukr.

GRAINSGILL
There are several places of this name and it means a ravine with a branch or fork. The elements are ON grein and ON gil.

GRANGE-OVER-SANDS
Barn for storing grain, belonging to Cartmel Priory. This is a Norman word, the meaning of which developed into 'farm'. The Grange in Borrowdale has the same meaning but belonged to Furness Abbey, who bought Borrowdale in the early 13th century for £160.

GRASMERE
From an early form Ceresmere 1203, the village of this name means lake with reeds or grass growing round the edge, from ON graes and ON maer. The tarn of this name means lake next to which pigs grazed, from ON gris, the earliest form being Grysemere 1374. The two place-names were once distinctly different but are now the same.

GRAYRIGG
Grey ridge from ON grar and ON hryggr. This hamlet, near Kendal, is on a limestone outcrop.

GRAYTHWAITE
Grey clearing, from ON grar and ON thveit.

GREAT DUN FELL
Large fortified hill. Great is Modern English. Dun is hill fort in Celtic. Fell is ON fjallr.

GREAT GABLE
The early form Mykelgavel 1338, shows ON mikill 'great' and ON gafl 'gavel'.

In Norway, gavl is recorded meaning 'a short mountain wall connecting two parallel mountain ridges'.

GREENODD
Green point or promontory, from ON groenn and ON oddr.

GREENSCOE
Green wood, from ON groenn and ON skogr.

GREENUP EDGE
Green slope, from ON groenn and ON hop. Edge has been added later.

GRETA
Stony river, from ON griot and ON a.

GREYSTOKE
A difficult etymology. Stoke is probably OE stoc which could mean 'monastery', 'place', or 'an area dependent on a manor', and indeed there is a Greystoke Hall here. 'Grey' could be Middle Irish craicc, or Welsh craig 'cliff'. There is here a limestone outcrop which could influence the name, eg ON grar stakkr 'grey pile of rocks'. Early forms Creistock 1167, Craystok 1292, Greystoks 1294 indicate the pronunciation of the time.

GREYSOUTHEN
Suthan's crag, from an Old Irish personal name Suthan, and Middle Irish craicc. This is an example of an inversion compound.

GRINSDALE
Grimr's valley, a Norse personal name with ON dalr as second element.

GRIZEBECK
Stream where pigs were kept, from ON gris and ON bekkr.

GRIZEDALE
Valley where pigs were kept, from ON gris and ON dalr. There are several valleys of this name.

GROFFA
Hollow hill, or hill where a stream comes forth. The first element is ON grof 'hole' or 'brook'. The second element is ON haugr 'hill'.

GROUND
After the dissolution of the monasteries, land was broken up into estates and

became known from the names of their new owners, for example Atkinson Ground, Dixon Ground, Jackson Ground etc.

GUMMERSHOW
Gunnarr's hill, the second element being ON haugr, and the first an ON personal name.

GUNNERKELD
Gunnarr's well. The second element is ON keldr, and the first a Norse personal name.

GUTTERBY
Godric's home, a Danish place-name.

H

HACKTHORPE
Village of a man called Haki. The second element is Old Danish thorp, so the first is probably a Danish personal name.

HAGS
There are several areas in Cumbria with this name, for example on high ground between Aldingham and Scales in Furness. It means broken moss ground, probably where peat was cut or timber hewn, from ON hogg 'gap'.

HALE
Nook or corner of land, from OE halh.

HARD KNOTT
Difficult hill, from ON harðr and ON knutr 'peak'. The nearby pass took its name from this hill, having been previously known as Wainscarth, a gap over which wagons could pass, from OE waegen and ON skarðr.

HARESCEUGH
Possibly hares' wood, from ON hari and ON skogr.

HARRINGTON
The farm of the descendants of Haefer, an OE personal name.

HARRISON STICKLE
OE sticol means steep. Harrison is obviously a person's name.

HARTER FELL
Fell where there are deer, the first word being 'hjortar', the genitive of ON hjortr 'deer'.

HARTLAW
Hjortr's hill, or deer hill, the second element being ON haugr.

HARTLEY
The various early forms do not give any real clue as to its meaning. Deer meadow is a possibility, from OE heort and OE leah.

HARTSOP
Deer valley, from ON hjortr and ON hop.

HAUSE
Neck of land, from ON hals.

HAVERFLATTS
Possibly flat land where oats were grown, from ON hafri and ON flatr, which although an adjective, was used as a noun after the 14th century.

HAVERIGG
Ridge where oats are grown, from ON hafri and ON hryggr. There is a possibility that the first element is ON hafr 'goat'.

HAVERTHWAITE
Clearing or field where oats are grown, from ON hafri and ON thveit.

HAWCOAT
Cottage or farm surrounded by a hedge, from OE cot and OE haga. This area was recorded as Hietun in Domesday Book, meaning 'high village'. Under the management of Furness Abbey from the 13th to the 15th centuries, cotes were established as sheep farms, eg Ireleth Cote, Walton Cote.

HAWESWATER
Hafr's water, from an ON personal name and ON vatn. The first element could be ON hafr 'goat'.

HAWKSDALE
Haukr's valley, from an ON personal name and ON dalr.

HAWKSHEAD
Haukr's shieling. The early forms are Hovkesete 1200 and Haukesset 1220, show the second element to be ON saetr 'shieling' and not ON hofuð 'head'.

HAWKSWELL
Haukr's well, from an ON personal name and OE wella.

HAWTHWAITE
Clearing on a hill, from ON haugr and ON thveit.

HAYCOCK
High lump or heap, from ON har and ON kokkr.

HAYSTACKS
The second element is ON stakki 'heap' or 'pile'. The first element could be ON har 'high' or a personal name Heggr.

HAZELSLACK
Valley with hazel trees, from ON hesli and ON slakkr.

HEGDALE
Heggr's valley, from an ON personal name and ON dalr.

HEGGERSCALE
Egil's hut, from an ON personal name and ON skali 'hut'.

HELBECK
Stream from a cave or hole, from ON hellir and ON bekkr.

HELM CRAG
Rock where there was a roofed shelter for cattle, from ON hialmr, compare Danish dialectal hjelm 'a kind of barn'.

HELSINGTON
Village of the dwellers on a neck of land, from OE hals 'neck of land' and OE ingatun. The first element could be a personal name, as in Helsfell, 3 miles north.

HELVELLYN
Obscure etymology. The name seems to be Celtic and the elements could be Welsh helfa 'hunting ground' and llyn 'lake'. Red Tarn east of the summit could have been a fishing lake (compare Angle Tarn), and presumably deer and small game could have been hunted on the fellside. The earliest form of the name, Helvillon 1577 is too late for positive identification.

HENSINGHAM
The home of Hensa's descendants, from an OE personal name, OE inga and OE ham.

HESKET
Horse race track, from ON hestaskeið.

HESKETH NEWMARKET
Horse race track as above. Newmarket, self-explanatory, would have been added later.

HEVERSHAM
Iofurr's home. The second element is ON heimr, later reformed by OE ham, and the first an ON personal name.

HIGH BIGGINS
High buildings. Compare Low Biggins nearby. Biggin is a dialect word meaning 'building'.

HIGH SPY HOWE
No doubt 'lookout hill', though there are no early forms. ON speja is a possible root, though the name looks comparatively modern, as though from ME espie. Howe is ON haugr 'hill'.

HIGH STREET
Mountain named after the road that ran along it. This is a modern name. It was previously known as Bretesstrete 'the Britons' road', showing that it was in use before the Romans came. The Romans used it to travel between their fort at Ambleside and Brocavum, at Penrith.

HINCASTER
? Heðinn's fort. OE caester means a Roman fort. Early forms Hennecastre, in Domesday Book, and Hanecaster 1260 are not a great help. There is an OE word henn 'wild bird', 'hen', which could mean that an abandoned fort was occupied by wild birds. Compare Outchester in Northumberland which means Roman fort occupied by owls.

HINDSCARTH
No early forms but probably 'mountain pass or gap where there are female deer', from ON hind and ON skarðr.

HOATHWAITE
Hollow clearing, from ON hol 'hollow' or 'deep' and ON thveit.

HOBCARTON
There is no satisfactory explanation for this name. The second element could be an Old Irish personal name Cartan.

HOFF
Temple or house, from ON or OE hof. This is a common place-name in Scandinavia, and could refer to a heathen temple.

HOLBECK
Deep stream, or stream issuing from a hole, from ON hol and ON bekkr.

HOLKER
Marsh with deep hollows, from ON hol and ON kjarr. The marshy shoreline is the same today.

HOLLINS
Holly trees, from ME holin. These were grown for feeding sheep in the winter.

HOLME
Island, from ON holmr. This place is situated amongst flat land near the river Bela.

HOLME CULTRAM
The island or raised land belonging to Culterham. The first word is ON holmr, as above. The first element of the second word is probably Celtic cul-tir 'narrow strip of land', and OE ham 'home'. This is an Irish inversion compound. An abbey once flourished here.

HOLMESCALES
Either Holmr's huts, or huts on a small island, from ON holmr and ON skali.

HONEYTHWAITE
Worthless or useless clearing, from ON unyt and ON thveit. This place-name is sometimes spelt Unithwaite.

HONISTER
An early form Unnisterre 1751, indicates that this is likely to mean Unni's summer pasture, the second element being ON saetr.

HOPESYKE
Ditch in a valley, from ON hop and ON sik.

HORNSBY
Ormr's house. The meaning of this is clear from an early form Ormesby 1210.

HOUGHTON
High farm, or farm on the spur of a hill, from OE hoh and OE tun.

HOUGUN
This place-name is now lost. It is mentioned in Domesday Book and has been successfully argued by Fred Barnes "Barrow and District" to have been the main manor of Furness, and also used as the name of the whole peninsula of Furness. It means 'among the hills' from the dative plural of ON haugr, haugum. It had previously been thought to have referred to Millom.

HOW
Hill, from ON haugr.

HOWGILL
Hill with a ravine, from ON haugr and ON gil.

HUGILL
Early forms Hogail 1256, and Hugayl 1274, seem to show this name to mean high path, from ON har and ON geil.

HUMPHREY HEAD
Hunfrið's headland, from an OE or ON personal name and either OE heafod or ON hofuð.

HUNSONBY
An early form Hunswanby, 1292, shows this name to mean dog keeper's home, from ON hundasveinn, and either ON byr or Old Danish by.

HUTTON
Farm on the spur of a hill, from OE hoh 'spur' and OE tun. Several places have this name, sometimes with a defining element coming second, for example, Hutton John, Hutton Roof, and Hutton-in-the-Forest.

I

ICKENTHWAITE
Clearing where there are squirrels, from ON ikorni and ON thveit.

ILL BELL
Bad, evil or difficult hill, from ON illr and probably Celtic moel. The second

element could be ON bjalla 'bell', referring to the shape of the hill. Either way it becomes ME belle.

ILL GHYLL
Bad or evil ravine, from ON illr and ON gil. The meaning of illr could be 'difficult or steep' when referring to topographical features.

INGLEWOOD
The wood of the English, from OE Engla and OE wudu. These would be Anglians who had travelled from the east of England.

INGS
Meadow, specially in a marshy place, from ON eng.

INTAKE
Land reclaimed from a moor, or enclosure, as in Rigg Intake, Broad Mire Intake, Moss Eccles Intake, from ON intaka.

IREBY
Home of the Irish, from OE Ira, genitive of the plural word Iras, and ON byr.

IRELETH
Hillside of the Irish, from OE Ira and ON or OE hlið 'slope'.

IRTHINGTON
Farm on the river Irthing, which is a British river name of unknown origin.

IRTON
Possibly farm of the Irish. However, this place is on the river Irt, an unexplained British name, so it could mean farm on the river Irt.

ISELL
Isi's meadow. The second element seems to be OE halh 'piece of flat land near a river', and the first a personal name.

IVE
This river name could possibly be from ON ifa 'yew'.

Place Names of Cumbria 47

Irton Road station on the Ravenglass to Eskdale railway.

Bridge over Newlands Beck, Uzzicar, south west of Keswick.

J

JOHNBY
Ion's or John's homestead, seemingly an English personal name with Old Danish by as second element.

K

KABER
An early form Kaberge, 1195, shows this name to mean jackdaw hill, from ON ka and ON berg.

KEARSTWICK
As is shown by the majority of the early forms, Kestwayte 1546, Keisthwaite 1640, for example, this name means clearing in a valley, from ON kjoss 'valley' and ON thveit.

KEEKLE BECK
Possibly 'winding' from an ON adjective kikall and ON bekkr 'stream'.

KELBARROW
Either spring by the mound, or Ketill's mound, from ON kelda and ON berg.

KELLETH
Either spring from a hillside, or Ketill's hillside, from ON kelda and ON hlið.

KELSICK
Either spring or well by a slow moving stream, from ON kelda, or Ketill's ditch, the second element being ON sic 'slow moving stream' or 'ditch'.

KENDAL
Valley of the river Kent which is a British river name Cunetio 'sacred stream', compare Caint in Anglesey and Cantia in northern France. The town was formerly known as Kirkby Kendal.

KENTMERE
Small lake on the river Kent. This was drained in the 1830s but another formed on the same site after the extraction of diatomite from the bed of the lake. The Kentmere reservoir at the head of the valley was built in 1848.

KEPPEL COVE
No early forms but probably 'horse ravine', from ON kapall and OE cofa.

KESWICK
This is the Scandinavianised form of OE Cesewic 'cheese farm' as in Chiswick. The second element is an early loan word from Latin vicus 'farm' or 'village'. As many names having 'wick' as a second element are found on or near Roman roads in Cumbria, it is fairly safe to assume that such a road passed through Keswick, though there is scant physical evidence. There must surely have been a connecting route between the Roman camp near Motherby and that at Caermote to the north of Bassenthwaite Lake, and it has been suggested that there was a link through Braithwaite over Whinlatter Pass to Cockermouth.

KIDSTY
There are no early forms but the name may mean Cydda's path, the second element being ON stigr.

KILLINGTON
The farm of Cylla's people, from OE Cylla and OE ingatun.

KINN
Head, headland, from Celtic ceann. The name of this prominent fell near Keswick is one of the few examples in this area of Goidelic Celtic, which developed into Gaelic and Erse. Most of the Celtic names in Cumbria are Brythonic, which was the basis for Welsh, Cornish and Breton. The equivalent of ceann in Brythonic Celtic is pen as in Penrith and Pennines.

KINNISIDE
OE Cyne's head (of valley), the second element being OE heafod.

KIRK
This is a very common element in place names and can mean either 'church' from ON kirkja, or 'circle' from OE circul, which is a Latin loan word. Originally the initial 'c' followed by 'i' or 'e' in OE would have been pronounced 'ch', so either the Latin pronunciation was retained, or the word circul was Scandinavianised in place names (see Keswick). There is a circular enclosure on Kirkby Moor named Kirk, and several other circles in Cumbria have Kirk in their names. However the issue is futher complicated as early Irish missionaries were urged to build churches on prehistoric sites, to defuse their influence and power.

KIRKANDREWS
St. Andrew's church, an inversion compound with ON kirkja as first element.

KIRKBARROW
Either church on a mound, from ON kirkja and OE beorg or ON berg, or a burial mound within a stone circle, from OE circul Scandinavianised and OE beorg. There are several remains of the latter on uncultivated moorland areas such as Burnmoor and Bleaberry Haws, dating from possibly Bronze Age. There are two places named Kirkbarrow within three miles of each other, west of Penrith.

KIRKBRIDE
St. Bride's church. Both this place-name and the one above are Irish inversion compounds.

KIRKBY
There are many names belonging to this group, which means home near the church, or village where there is a church, from ON kirkiubyr. Kirkby Kendal, Kirkby Ireleth, Kirkby Lonsdale, are named after locations. Kirkby Stephen is named after an abbot Stephanus, and Kirkby Thore from an early owner Thorir, an ON personal name. When the place name Kirkby occurs without association with a church it is possible that the name could mean 'home by the circle'.

KIRKCAMBECK
Either church or circle on a crooked stream, from ON kirkja, or Scandinavianised OE circul, and Celtic cambaco 'a crooked stream'.

KIRK FELL
Possibly 'circle fell' from OE circul, Scandinavianised. Although there are many 'piles of stones' marked on the Ordnance Survey map on this mountain in Wasdale which could have once been circles, it seems more likely that this mountain was so named after its unusually conical shape. There is another fell of this name further to the north, of a similar shape.

KIRKLAND
There are several places of this name. The two possible meanings are 'land belonging to a church' which is certainly true of the hamlet east of Penrith, or 'land with a circle'.

KIRKOSWALD
The church of St. Oswald, who was an Irish saint.

KIRKSANTON
Possibly St. Sanctan's church, an Irish saint. Both this place-name and the one above are Irish inversion compounds. However, as there have been three large stone circles here, the name of one of which was Kirkstones, it is also possible that Kirksanton could have lost a 't' and the name could mean 'home by the

stone circle' from OE circul, OE stan and OE tun. The early forms do not give any evidence of this, however.

KIRKSTEADS
Site by the church. This name has been Scandinavianised from OE ciricstede.

KIRKSTONE PASS
Probably stone circle pass, from OE circul Scandinavianised and OE stan. Here the circle is at Hird's Wood 2 miles north of Troutbeck. There could have been other circles now destroyed.

KNAPETHORN
Either Knapi's thorn bush, or thorn bush on a knoll, from OE cnaepp 'hilltop' and OE thorn.

KNIPE
Steep overhanging rock, from ON gnipa.

KNOCK
Hillock, from Old Irish cnocc.

KNOUTBERRY
Possibly rocky hill, from ON knottr and ON berg.

L

LADYHOLME
Island of Our Lady. St. Mary's hermitage was here, mentioned in 1272.

LAITHES
Barns, from ON hlaða.

LAMBRIGG
Lambi's ridge, or lambs' ridge, from ON lambi and ON hryggr.

LAMONBY
Home of Lambert, or Langbein, a nickname meaning long legs.

LAMPLUGH
An old Cumbrian name corresponding to Welsh llanplwy meaning 'the church of the parish'.

LANERCOST
The first element is either Celtic llanerch 'clearing, glade' or Celtic llan 'enclosure, church', but the second element is obscure.

LANGDALE
Long valley, from ON lang and ON dalr.

LANGRIGG
Long ridge, from ON lang and ON hryggr.

LANGSTRATH
Long valley, from ON lang and Goidelic Celtic strath.

LANGWATHBY
Homestead by the long ford, from ON lang, ON vaðr, and ON byr. The ford here on the River Eden is still visible beside the single lane iron bridge which now spans the water.

LANTY'S TARN
A personal name which is the diminutive of Lancelot, and ON tjorn.

LATRIGG
Ridge with an animal's lair, from ON latr and ON hryggr.

LATTERBARROW
Hill with animals' lairs, from ON latar, plural of latr, and ON berg, or OE beorg.

LAVERSDALE
Leofhere's valley, from an OE personal name and ON dalr. There was an OE word dael 'valley' which was in widespread use, but in Scandinavian areas dale is usually of Norse or Danish origin.

LAZONBY
A freedman's home, from ON leysingr and ON byr.

LEATH
A long hill slope, from ON hlið.

LEECE
Glades in sparse woods, from the plural of OE leah.

LEGBURTHWAITE
There are no early forms but the meaning probably is the clearing by Leggr's home, from ON Leggr, ON byr and ON thveit.

LEVEN
This is a British river name meaning 'smooth', from Celtic llyfn.

LEVENS
A contraction of Levenness 'smooth even headland' from Celtic llyfn and ON nes. This is a particularly flat valley.

LEVERS WATER
The meaning of this name is obscure. It could be from a personal Norse name Leifi, or a British river name Laefer, modern Welsh Llafar, 'noisy', 'resounding'. The tarn was first dammed in 1840 to increase the water supply for the copper mines below. There is a spectacular waterfall from the tarn now and there must also have been one in former times which would have provided the noise.

LICKBARROW
Corpse mound, from OE lic and OE beorg. This presumably refers to a burial mound but there is no trace of the tumulus there now.

LIDDEL
Valley with long sloping sides, from ON hlið and ON dalr.

LINDAL
Valley with lime trees, from ON lind and ON dalr.

LINDALE
As above. Lime or linden trees may be a different kind of tree from modern limes. ON lind is probably related to Greek elate 'silver fir', a tree which would be more likely to grow in this area.

LINDETH
Lime tree hill, from ON lind and ON hofuð.

LING HOLME
Heather island, from ON lyng and ON holmr.

LINGLOW
Heather covered hill. The second element seems to be OE hlaw 'hill'.

LINGMELL
Heather covered hill. The second element is Celtic moel 'hill'.

LITTLE ARROW MOOR
There are no early forms, but this could mean 'on the hillside', from Celtic ar 'on' and rhiw 'hill slope'. The self-explanatory little and moor would have been added later. This area, about a thousand feet below the summit of Coniston Old Man has many remains of early habitation from settlements to tumuli. Another explanation could be 'at the shieling', from the dative singular of ON erg.

LIZA
Bright river, from ON ljos and ON a.

LODORE
Lower gap, from ME laghedure 'lower door'. There was also a heghedure 'a higher door or gap' further up the valley now known as High Lodore.

LOPPERGARTH
Vagabond's enclosure, from ON hlaupari and ON garðr.

LORTON
Farm on the Hlora, which is probably a Norse name like Lora in Norway meaning 'roaring', an old name for the river Whitbeck.

LOUGHRIGG
Probably ridge by the tarn, from a Celtic word lough and ON hryggr. Compare Scottish loch and Irish lough.

LOWESWATER
Leafy lake, from ON lauf 'leaf' and ON saer 'lake'. 'Water' would have been added later.

LOWICK
Leafy creek, from ON lauf and ON vik. The river Crake at this point is still overhung by large trees.

LOWTHER
Probably foaming river, from ON lauðr 'froth' and ON a 'river'.

LUNE
Health giving one, from a Celtic root lon. This river gives its name to Lonsdale, Lancaster, and Lancashire.

LYTH
Long sloping hillside, from ON hlið. This valley near Windermere is well-known nowadays for its damson trees.

LYVENNET
A British river name, possibly meaning smooth stream. The first element is probably the same as Leven 'smooth'. The second element could be Celtic nant, which means 'brook', 'ravine', or 'valley'. There is much evidence of British settlement in this valley to the east of Shap.

M

MAIDEN MOOR
No early forms, but this is possibly a Celtic name meaning 'fort of stones', from Celtic meini, plural of maen, 'stones', and Celtic dun 'fort'. There is a faint chance that the first element could be a personal name Mai, which was also the name of a Celtic goddess. The shape of the summit of this hill near Keswick suggests that it could well have been fortified. Maiden castles were the names given to early earthworks throughout Britain. There are two known 1st century BC circular ramparted probable homesteads in Cumbria, one just to the north of Ullswater, and the other on Burnmoor between Eskdale and Wastwater known as maiden castle. See also Mayburgh, below.

MALLERSTANG
Either Malfrith's spit of land, from Malfrið's tangi, or pole on a bare hill, from Welsh moelfre and ON stongr.

MANSERGH
The shieling of Mani, from an ON personal name and ON erg. This was spelt Manzsergh in Domesday Book.

MANSRIGGS
Either ridge where killings took place, from ON manslagari 'homicide', and ON hryggr, or Mani's ridge.

MARDALE
Either boundary mark valley, from ON maeri and ON dalr or lake valley, from ON marr and ON dalr. There are three lakes in this valley, Blea Water, Small Water, and Haweswater, which was enlarged in 1937 as a reservoir drowning the village of Mardale. In times of drought the remains of the village can still be seen.

MARTINDALE
St. Martin's valley. A cross dedicated to St. Martin stood in the valley before 1266.

MARTON
Farm by a small lake, from OE mere and tun.

MARYPORT
A modern name, after the wife of the builder of the harbour in 1750-60. There was an old place-name, Ellensfoote, meaning the mouth of the river Ellen.

MATTERDALE
Possibly valley where madder grew, which was a climbing plant from which a yellow dye was made. From ON maðra and ON dalr.

MAUGHONBY
Merchiaun's home, from a Celtic personal name and ON byr.

MAULDS MEABURN
The first name is Maud the wife of William de Veteriponte. The second name is probably stream in a meadow from OE maed 'meadow' and OE burna 'stream'.

MAYBURGH
Maiden castle, from OE maege and OE burg. This is the name of ancient circular remains near Penrith which has several standing stones at its centre.

MEAL BANK
Bank with sandy soil, from ON melr.

MEALRIGG
Either middle ridge, the old spelling of which was recorded as Midelrig in 1189, or sandy ridge from ON melr and ON hryggr.

MEALY SYKE
Ditch or slow moving stream by a sand bank, from ON melr and syk.

MEASAND
Narrow water or channel, from ON mjosund.

MEATHOP
Either valley with sandy soil, from ON melr and ON hop, or middle valley, from ON meðal and ON hop.

A well established footpath on Claife Heights, west of Windermere.

MELBECKS
Sand bank between streams from ON melr, and ON bekkr.

MELDON HILL
Fortified hill, from Celtic moel 'hill' and Celtic dun 'fort'. Many of these Pennine hills overlooking the Eden Valley were fortified.

MELKINTHORPE
Irish name Maelchon's village. The second element is Old Danish thorp.

MELL
As in Great Mell Fell and Little Mell Fell, a hill, from Celtic moel 'bare hill'.

MELMERBY
Either Melmor's home, an Old Irish name meaning St. Mary's servant, or home in the sandy field, from ON melr and ON byr.

MICKELDORE
A large pass, from ON mikill and ON dor. Compare Lodore.

MICKELTHWAITE
A large clearing, from ON mikill and ON thveit.

MIDDLESCEUGH
Middle wood from OE middel and OE sceaga.

MILBURN
Mill stream, from OE mylen burna.

MILLNESS
Promontory by the mill, from OE mylen and OE ness.

MILLOM
At the mills, from an OE dative plural mylenum. These most probably were windmills, as records state that they existed in England before the 12th century. Hand mills were known as querns.

MILLTHROP
Village by the mill, from OE mylen and Old Danish thorp, showing metathesis of the 'r'.

MILNTHORPE
Village by the mill, from OE mylen and Old Danish thorp.

MILTON
Farm by the mill, from OE mylen and OE tun.

MINT
The name of this river north east of Kendal is of British origin, from the root mim- 'to make a sound'. Mint House is mentioned in Domesday Book as Mimet.

MIRKBOOTHS
Dark huts from ON mirkr and ON buð.

MIRKHOLME
Dark island from ON mirkr and ON holmr.

MISLET
The early form Michelesletta shows that the name could mean 'Michael's slope'. Michael could be Michael le Fleming who assisted William the Conquerer, and after the conquest was sent north to fight the Scots. As a reward he was given many noble estates in Furness. In Earl Stephen's Charter in the 12th Century the lands belonging to Sir Michael were named as such to distinguish them from those owned by Furness Abbey.

MITERDALE
Valley of the river Mite, which shows a Scandinavian genitive on a British name.

MOCKERKIN TARN
An early form Moldcorkin 1292, seems to show an Irish inversion compound meaning Corcan's bare hill, from Old Irish maol and an Irish personal name Corc, with the diminutive -an suffix. Mockerkin Tarn was known as Tarn Meran in the 14th century.

MONK CONISTON
Part of the land near Coniston Water that belonged to the monks of Furness Abbey.

MOORTHWAITE
Moorland clearing, from OE mor and ON thveit.

MOOTA HILL
Meeting place hill, from OE or ON mot and ON haugr.

MORESBY
Home of Maurice, a French name. By is probably Old Danish.

MORICAMBE
Crooked estuary, from Celtic moryd 'estuary' and Celtic cam 'bent' or 'crooked'. Morecambe has the same meaning.

MORLAND
Land on the moor, from OE morland.

MOSEDALE
Mossy or boggy valley, from ON mosi and ON dalr.

MOSSER
Mossy or boggy shieling, from ON mosi and ON erg.

MOTHERBY
Moðir's home. This is a Danish personal name which does mean 'mother'. 'By' is also Danish.

MUNCASTER
Either Mula's fortified enclosure, or fort on a headland, from ON muli, a headland or promontory, and Latin castra, an early loan word. The Roman fort here, Clanoventa, was taken over by later settlers.

MUNGRISDALE
Mungo's valley for pigs, from ON gris and ON dalr. The tiny church in this hamlet is named after St. Kentigern, also known as Mungo from Celtic Mynghu. He was Bishop of Glasgow in about 550 AD and journeyed through north Cumbria preaching, converting and baptising. Other churches bear his name, such as those in Irthington, Grinsdale, Kirkland, Bromfield, Aspatria, Caldbeck, Castle Sowerby and Crosthwaite (Keswick).

MURRAH
Early forms such as Mowra 1292, show this name to mean corner on a moor, from OE mor and ON vra.

MURTON
Farm on a moor, from OE mor and OE tun.

MUSGRAVE
Either mossy or boggy dug land, from ON mosi, and the past participle of OE graben, or grove frequented by mice, from OE or ON mus and OE graf. The second element could be ON gryfia 'hole or pit'.

N

NAB
A promontory, from OE neb 'beak' or 'protuberance'. Compare nob, nib and nub.

NADDALE
Either point or wedge in a valley, from ON naddr and ON dalr, or snake valley, from ON naðr 'adder'.

NAN BIELD PASS
Pass of the shelter, from Gaelic na-n 'of the' and bield which is a Scottish and Northern English word meaning shelter.

NATEBY
Nati's home. This seems more likely than nuts storehouse from ON hnata and byr, or cattleshed, from ON naut and byr.

NATLAND
Early forms Natalund, 1175, and Natalunt, 1246, seem to indicate that this name means Nata's grove, from ON lundr rather than land.

NETHERBY
Lower farmhouse from ON neðarr and byr.

NETHERTON
Lower farmstead, from ON neðarr and ON tun.

NETTLESLACK
Nettle valley from ON netla and slakki.

NEWBIGGIN
New building or house, from ON byggia, to build. Biggin is a Cumbrian dialect word for a building.

NEWBY
New homestead, from ON nyr and ON byr.

NEWLANDS
Newly cleared land, or newly acquired land. The Newlands Valley near Keswick was so named when a shallow lake named Husaker was drained to form agricultural land in the 12th century.

NEWTON
New homestead. This is probably the most common English place-name.

NEWTON ARLOSH
The first name as above. Arlosh, originally Arlock, possibly means 'on land cleared by burning', from British ar 'on' and llosg 'burnt ground'.

NEWTON REIGNY
The first name as above. The second part of the name is a personal name. In 1212 it is stated in a charter that the land was given by Henry I to Thurstan de Reingny.

NIBTHWAITE
Clearing with a new hut, from ON nyr and buð, and thveit.

NINE STANDARDS
These early man-made pillars are situated on high moorland to the south east of Kirkby Stephen. They are probably boundary marks or an early form of signpost. The word standard means an upright pillar, from the ME word standard derived from Old French estandard.

NOOK
Corner, from Gaelic Irish niuk, which is from a Scandinavian variant neuk.

NORTHSCEUGH
North wood, from ON norð, and ON skogr.

O

OAKSHAW
Oak wood, from OE ac and OE scaga.

OLD MAN
Old cairn or pile of stones, from a Celtic word 'maen'. The first element could be Celtic allt 'hill'. There used to be three large cairns on the summit of this mountain near Coniston. There is another Old Man on the summit of a hill called Knock in the Pennines.

ORGRAVE
A place where ore has been dug, from OE ora and OE graef.

ORMATHWAITE
An early form Northmanethwait 1260, shows this name to mean 'clearing of the Northmen' or 'Norse'. The name Northman survived until the 14th century when it became Norman.

ORMSGILL
Ormr's ravine. This is a common personal name in ON. As a common noun it means worm, serpent, or dragon. The second element is ON gil.

ORMSIDE
Ormr's hill, the second element probably being ON hofuð, rather than ON saetr, a summer pasture.

ORREST
Battle, from ON orrosta. It has been speculated that as this place-name is on a probable junction of two Roman roads, there could have been a battle here. It is known that Eadmund fought Duvenald (Dunmail) in 945, that Earl Thored from York harried Westmorland in 966, and that Aethelred the Unready ravaged Cumberland in 1000, to drive out the Norse.

ORTON
Farmstead higher up, from ON ofarr and tun, or farmstead on the river bank, from OE ofer and tun. The first element however could be OE ora 'boundary mark', or OE ora 'ore'.

OUGHTERSIDE
Uhtred's shieling, the second element being ON saetr, and the first an ON personal name.

OULTON
Ulfr's farm. Ulfr was a common ON personal name. As a common noun it means wolf.

OUSBY
Ulfr's home, as is shown by the old form Ulvesbi, from a Scandinavian personal name and Old Danish by.

OUTHGILL
Ulfr's ravine. The second element is ON gil.

OUTHWAITE
Ulfr's clearing. The second element is ON thveit.

OVERBY
Farm higher up, from ON ofarr and byr. It is very difficult to distinguish between ON byr and Old Danish by.

OXENHOLME
Island or restricted area where oxen were kept, from OE oxa in the plural oxen, and ON holmr.

OXEN PARK
One of the enclosures ordered by the Abbot of Furness, by licence from Edward I, to increase the number of tenants who would pay rent to Furness Abbey. Stot Park and Abbot Park were other abbey enclosures.

P

PAPCASTLE
Priest's or bishop's castle, from OE papa and OE castel, both elements being Latin loan words. It has been suggested that the name means Pipard's Castle after Gilbert Pipard. He was the husband of Alice de Romilly who inherited this area of Allerdale. There was a Roman fort here.

PARKAMOOR
Moor with paddocks, from OE pearroca and OE mor.

PARROCK
Paddock, from OE pearroca.

PARTON
Probably farm in an enclosure, from OE pearroca and OE tun.

PATTERDALE
Patrick's valley, which although it is the name of an Irish saint, does not necessarily mean that St. Patrick visited this valley.

PAVEY ARK
No early forms but ark is probably ON erg 'shieling'. It is possible that pavey is Norman French pavée meaning a prepared path.

PENN
Hill, from Celtic pen. This fell in Dunnerdale is in the heart of British settlements.

PENNINGTON
Probably the hamlet of the descendants of Pinna, which could be from the Welsh penaig 'chieftain'. There is evidence of early occupation around this hamlet on the Furness peninsula, such as an enclosure known as The Castle, and a burial mound beneath which it is rumoured lies the body of Lord Ella with his golden sword. (See Ellerbarrow). Another proposal for the meaning of this name is 'farm paying a penny rent'.

PENNY BRIDGE
This bridge over the River Crake is named after a local family, Penny.

PENRITH
Red hill, from Celtic pen 'hill' and Celtic rhudd 'red' referring to the sandstone outcrop on which the town is built.

PENRUDDOCK
Small red hill, from Celtic pen 'hill' and Celtic rhudd and a diminutive oc, as in hillock and tussock. There is a dialectal word ruddock meaning 'redbreast'. This hamlet, five miles from Penrith, appears to stand on an outcrop of red sandstone.

PIEL ISLAND
The ruined castle on this island was a pele tower built by the monks of Furness Abbey to protect their port at Roa Island. The original name of the island was Fouldrey, the etymology of which is dubious; it could mean bird island like Foulney nearby.

PILLAR
Probably pointed hill, from ON pil and ON haugr. This refers to the famous needle of rock on the mountain of the same name.

PLUMPTON
Farmstead where plum trees grow, from OE plume and OE tun.

PONSONBY
Puncun's homestead. John the son of Puncun mentioned in 1177 was the owner of Ponsonby.

POOLEY BRIDGE
Pool by the hill, from OE pol and OE hlaw. The river Eamont runs past the foot of Dunmallard Hill, an Iron Age fort, at this point. The word bridge would have been added later.

PORTINSCALE
Prostitute's hut. The first element is OE portcwen, and the second element is ON skali. However, Carole Hough has argued (EPNS, Journal 29, 1996-97, "The Ladies of Portinscale") that the first element could mean merely towns-women, as opposed to those of ill-repute. She reasons that as this name is the sole reference to prostitution among all the place-names of England, it has to be treated with caution.

PRESTON PATRICK
Patrick's priest's village or parsonage. This is an Irish name and an Irish word order.

PUDDING STONE
There are several large rocks in Cumbria with this name, which must refer to their round shape. A pudding was originally animals' intestines stuffed with meat and grain. Robbie Burns referred to the haggis as 'Great Chieftain o' the puddin' race'.

Q

QUARLES
Circles, from OE hwerfles the plural of hwerfel. Stone circles were probably found in this area but are no longer to be seen.

QUERNBARROW
This name was originally Quernberg meaning mill (on the) hill, or hill where millstones came from, from ON kvern and ON berg. ON kvern could mean a millstone or a hand mill.

QUERNMORE
Moor where millstones were quarried, from either ON kvern or OE cweorn and OE or ON mor.

R

RABY
Farmstead at a boundary, from ON ra and ON byr, which suggests perhaps an administrative role.

It is most unusual to find three single element place-names on one signpost.

RAISEBECK
Stream next to a cairn, from ON hreysi and ON bekkr.

RAISETHWAITE
Clearing where there is a cairn, from ON hreysi and ON thveit.

RAKE
Path for sheep which usually cuts across a steep hillside, for example Lady's Rake, Jack's Rake, Yorkshire Rake, from ON rak.

RAKESMOOR
Moor across which there is a path for sheep or cattle, from ON rak and ON mor.

RAMPSHOLM
Either Hrafn's islet, or islet of wild garlic, from OE hramsa, and ON holmr.

RAMPSIDE
Either Hrafn's summer pasture from a Norse personal name and ON saetr, or ram's head, from OE ramm and OE heafod, naming a spit of land resembling a ram's head. The former explanation seems more likely.

RANDAL HOLME
Possibly strip of unploughed land in a valley, from OE or ON rand and ON dalr. Rand can also mean edge or border. Holmr means islet or a strip of isolated land different from the surroundings.

RASETT
Hill pasture or shieling on a boundary, from ON ra and ON saetr. The first element could be ON vra, in which case the name would mean shieling in a corner.

RATHMOSS
Fort by marshy ground, from Old Irish rath and OE mos. The neighbouring farm Rathvale has the same first element. Traces of the fort are still visible on the summit of nearby Shooting House Hill, Kirkby Moor. Ireleth (q.v.) is 2 miles to the south-west.

RAUGHTON
Farm on Roe Beck, which means boundary stream, from ON ra and ON a as the first element and ON tun.

RAVENGLASS
Probably a British name, from Celtic reanna 'promontories', or Gaelic rann 'division, boundary', and glas 'stream'. Early forms were Rengles 1170, and

Reynglas 1250. The first element could have been reformed by Norse settlers to a personal name Hrafnkell. The Romans used this now silted up harbour, but called it Clanoventa.

RAVENSTONEDALE
Valley of Hrafn's stone, or possibly a personal name Hrafnsteinn, and ON dalr.

RAVENSTY
Either Hrafn's path, or path where ravens collect. The second element is ON stigr meaning path.

REAGILL
Possibly fox valley, from ON refr and ON gil.

REDMAIN
Early forms Redeman, 1184, and Rademan, 1202, seem to show that this place means red stone or cairn, from OE read or Celtic rhud and Celtic maen.

RENWICK
Hrafn's farm, or farm on river Raven, as shown by the early form Ravenswich 1178. The second element is OE wic, and the village lies on a Roman road.

RESTON
Farm amongst brushwood, from OE hris and OE tun. Early forms Rispetun 1272, and Respeton 1297, show the first element to have been originally an unrecorded OE word cognate with Old High German hrispahi 'brushwood'.

RHEGED
A 6th century kingdom covering Lancashire, Cumberland and Galloway with Carlisle as its chief city. It was ruled by Urien, a powerful leader, who led a coalition of British kings against invading Angles.

RIGGINDALE
Probably valley of the ridges, from ON hryggena, the genitive plural of hryggr 'ridge', and ON dalr. There are pronounced ridges on either side of this valley near Haweswater.

RISE HILL
Hill with a cairn, from ON hreysi.

ROA ISLAND
Red island, from ON rauðr and ON ey, but early forms are lacking. Iron ore which stained the ground red was shipped from here from early times.

ROANHEAD
Red headland, from ON rauðr and ON hofuð. This derivation is supported by the early form Rohad in the 14th century and the red colour from the haematite mined here remains to this day. A later form, Roundhead, from documents concerning rent for Furness Abbey in the 16th century, not only shows the pronunciation of the vowel of the first element to be 'ow' which would support the derivation from rauðr, but also explains how the 'n' finds its way into the name.

ROBINSON
This hill near Buttermere was part of the land bought at the Dissolution by Richard Robinson.

ROCKBY
Hrokr's home. The second element is either ON byr or Old Danish by, and the first a Scandinavian personal name.

ROCKCLIFFE
Red cliff, from ON rauðr, and ON klif.

ROOSE
Marsh or plain, from British rhos. There was a village called Rosse on the Furness peninsula which was washed away by the sea.

ROSGILL
Horse ravine, from ON hros and ON gil. Wild ponies still roam Rosgill Moor, near Shap.

ROSSET
Summer pasture where horses were kept, from ON hros and ON saetr.

ROSTHWAITE
Early forms Rasethwate 1503, and Raystwhat show this name means clearing marked by a cairn, from ON hreysi and ON thveit.

ROTHAY
Loud sounding river, from ON rautand, the present participle of the verb rauta 'to make a noise', and ON a 'river'. Etymologically it is possible that this name means red river, from ON rauðr and ON a, but topographically it is not. It is a broad swift river running from Grasmere to Windermere and dominates Rydal valley.

ROTTINGTON
Home of the descendants of Rota, derived from OE rot 'merry'.

ROUNDTHWAITE
Clearing of the mountain ash, from ON raun in the genitive singular raunar and ON thveit.

ROUTENBECK
Stream making a loud noise, from ON rautand, the present participle of the verb rauta, which means to make a loud noise, and ON a 'river'. The final element is ON bekkr 'stream', probably added later. Compare Rothay above.

ROWE HEAD
Red hill, from ON rauðr and ON hofuð. Rich deposits of haematite have made the soil red in this area of Furness.

ROWRAH
Early forms Rucwrabec 1248 and Rukwra show the name to mean 'corner where rye was grown', from Old Scandinavian rug 'rye' and ON vra 'corner'.

RULBUTH
Hrolf's hut. The second element is ON buð, and the first an ON personal name.

RUSLAND
Hrolf's land. The first recording of this name, Rolesland in 1336 disproves any theory that the first element could be from ON hros 'horse'.

RUTHWAITE
Clearing where rye was grown, from ON rugr 'rye'. However the first element could be ON hruðr 'scurf, scruff' in the sense of rough ground.

RYDAL
Probably 'valley of the Rothay', a contraction of ON rautand, ON a, and ON dalr. An early form Ridale 1240 is of no help, but the early form of Rydal Water is (see below). Other place-name researchers, in particular Eilert Ekwall, propose this name to mean valley where rye was grown, from OE ryge or ON rugr and OE dael or ON dalr.

RYDAL MOUNT
The home of William Wordsworth for 30 years after his marriage to Mary Hutchinson. The 'mount' is a supposedly 9th century mound in the garden where beacons would have been lit to warn of approaching enemies.

RYDAL WATER
Lake of the river Rothay, from its early form Routhemere, 1275.

S

SAD GILL
Ravine with a shieling, from ON saetr and ON gil.

SALES
Pools or puddles, from ON seyla.

SALKELD
Early forms Salcheld 1100, and Salighild 1242, show the name to mean sallow wood. The first element is OE salh 'sallow' which is a low growing shrub of the genus Salix, and OE hylte 'wood'. Great and Little Salkeld were originally a royal manor held by Ranulf Meschin.

SANDFORD
Sandy ford, from OE sand and OE ford.

SANDGATE
Sand path, from ON sandr and ON gata. This was the start of the way from Cartmel peninsula across Leven Sand to Conishead.

SANDWATH
Sandy ford, from ON sandr and ON vaðr.

SANDWICK
This place on the east shore of Ullswater means sandy creek, from ON sandr and ON vik.

SANDWITH
Wood on sandy ground from ON sandr and ON viðr. As this place to the south of Whitehaven is not on a stream, it is unlikely that the second element is ON vaðr 'ford'.

SANTON
Hamlet on sandy ground, from ON sandr and ON tun.

SATTERHOW
Hill with huts, from ON saetar (plural of saetr) and ON haugr.

SATTERTHWAITE
Shielings, or summer huts in a clearing, from ON saetar and ON thveit.

SAWREY
Shieling in muddy land, from ON saurr 'mud, poor soil' and ON erg.

SCAFELL
Either hill with a hut, from ON skali and ON fjall, or hill with a bald crown from ON skalli. This is the highest mountain in Cumbria and its summit is rocky and bare of vegetation, so the second explanation could be the correct one.

SCALEBY
Hut used as a dwelling place, from ON skali and ON byr.

SCALES
Huts, from ON skali.

SCALTHWAITERIGG
Hut in a clearing on a ridge, from ON skali, ON thveit and ON hryggr.

SCANDALE
There are no early forms but the meaning could be 'limited valley', from ON skamt and ON dalr.

SCARTH
Gap, from ON scarð.

SCAWDALE
Valley with a hut, from ON skali and ON dalr.

SCEUHEAD
Top of a wood, from OE sceaga, or ON skogr, and OE heafod, or ON hofuð.

SCOAT FELL
Fell with projecting ridge, from ON skuti and ON fjallr.

SCOUT SCAR
A jutting out rock, from ON skuti 'prominent rock' and ON sker 'crag'.

SCREES
Mass of detritus on a mountainside, from ON skriða 'landslip'.

SCRITHWAITE
Clearing by a landslip on a hillside, from ON skriða, and ON thveit.

SEASCALE
Hut by the sea, from ON saer and ON skali.

SEATALLAN
This name possibly means Alein's shieling, from a personal name and ON saetr. The element saetr is usually found last in a place-name except when it is in the plural form, as in Satterthwaite, or when it is attached to a personal name, which is an Irish inversion compound.

SEAT SANDAL
Sandulf's shieling, the first word being ON saetr. The order of these words shows an Irish influence.

SEATHWAITE
Clearing by a lake, from ON saer, and ON thveit. There are two places with this name. Seathwaite in Dunnerdale was named after Seathwaite Tarn nearby: Seathwaite in Borrowdale now has no tarn nearby, but from evidence of the first element and of the first element of Seatoller (see below) it seems likely that there was a small lake here, now drained. Maps of the area show drainage ditches and the unusually straight line of the river Derwent here, with a man made embankment, would seem to show man's intervention in the geography of upper Borrowdale.

SEATOLLER
Etymology dubious. It is possible that the Celtic talar 'headland' is the second element to which ON saer 'lake', 'body of water', was prefixed at a later date. There is a pronounced promontory here in Borrowdale which deflects the river Derwent, itself a Celtic name, so the meaning would be 'promontory by the lake'. There is a possibility that the name could mean Thorleif's lake, in which case the word order suggests an Irish influence. Dr. Diana Whaley of Newcastle University, has proposed that the first element of this name and the preceding one, is ON saetr (with the second element of this name being ON alor 'alder tree') in Nomina 1996. However, it is most unusual to have a usually second element, saetr, as a first element unless it is in the plural, such as Satterthwaite, or accompanied by a personal name in an inversion compound, such as Seat Sandal.

SEATON
Hamlet by the sea or lake, from ON saer and ON tun. There are two places of this name, both being near the sea.

SEBERGHAM
Possibly home on the flat topped hill, from ON setberg and ON heimr.

SEDBERGH
Flat-topped hill, from ON setberg. There are places of the same name in Iceland and Norway. This one was mentioned in Domesday Book as Sedbergt.

SEDGEWICK
The farm of Siggi, a Norse name and a Latin loan word vicus which becomes OE wic. This place is near a Roman road and the Roman fort of Alone, just south of Kendal.

SELKER
Probably willow marsh, from ON selja 'willow' and ON kjar.

SELLA
Probably willow hill, or hut on a hill, from ON sel 'hut' and ON haugr 'hill'.

SELLAFIELD
No early forms, but the first part could be as above. It is strange to see the modern nuclear power station here almost next to a primitive stone circle (which had been destroyed but was reconstructed by local people).

SELSIDE
Willow shieling, from ON selja and ON saetr. The first element could be a personal name Seli.

SERGEANT MAN
No early forms. The second element is Celtic man 'cairn'. The first element could possibly be road or path from Welsh sarn.

SERGEANT'S CRAG
This refers to a local family of William Sargyante 1602.

SETTERAH
Huts on the summer pasture, from ON saetar and ON erg.

SEWBORWENS
Seven burial mounds, from OE seofan and OE burgaesn. Several long cairns remain to this day near this farm to the north west of Penrith.

SHAP
The early forms, Heppa 1220, Yhep 1234, indicate this name is from OE heap, which means not only a hill or pile of stones in a circle, but also a gathering of people. It has been suggested that Shap was a 'thingwall', or parliament meeting place.

SHEFFIELD PIKE
This is probably a corruption of sheep fold, from OE sceap and OE fald. OE pic 'peak' is the second word.

SHOULTHWAITE
An early form Heolthwaitis 1280 shows this name to mean circle field, from ON hjol and ON thveit, referring to a stone circle. This hamlet is 2 miles south of the Castlerigg stone circle near Keswick.

SILECROFT
Willow field, from ON selja and OE croft 'field'.

SILLOTH
Barn by the sea, from ON saer and ON hlaða.

SINKFALL
Hollow in the ground, from ?ON which becomes ME senk 'depression '.

SIZERGH
The shieling of Sigriðr. The first element is a woman's name, and the second is ON erg.

SKALDERSKEW
Skjaldvor's wood. This is a woman's name. The second element is ON skogr.

SKEGGLESWATER
An early form Skakelswatre 1375 shows this to mean Skakul's tarn. Skakul is an ON personal name.

SKELGHYLL
Roaring water in the ravine, from ON skjallr from an earlier skella which is an adjective meaning 'resounding' .

SKELLS
There are several places around Urswick with the element skel, such as Skelmore and Skeldon. It could mean ledge, from a dialectal word skelf, related to OE scylfe. This would suit the limestone topography. However there is a possibility that this name could mean shells, from ON skel in the plural, and would refer to ancient middens left by shellfish eating people, discovered by the Norse. Morecambe Bay, well known for its shellfish, is 2 miles east of Urswick.

Hartsop Beck tumbles down Dovedale, in Patterdale. Hartsop means 'deer valley'.

SKELSMERGH
Skjaldmarr's shieling. Skjaldmarr is an ON personal name and shieling is from ON erg.

SKELTON
Probably farm on a ledge or ridge, from a dialectal word skelf, related to OE scylfe, and OE tun.

SKELWITH
Ford by the loud sounding water. The second element is ON vaðr 'ford', and the first is ON skella.

SKETTLE GILL
Asketil's ravine. The second element is ON gil, and the first a Norse personal name.

SKIDDAW
There are no early forms of this mountain name. The second element is ON haugr 'mountain'. The first element could be ON skeiðr 'racecourse' (compare Racecourse Hill on High Street), and the eastern flanks are flat enough for this to be a possibility. Another possible first element is ON skuti 'projecting rock', or even ON skyti 'archers'.

SKIRWITH
Either bright ford, from ON skirr and ON vaðr, or district wood, from OE scir 'district', 'shire', Scandinavianised to skir and ON viðr 'wood'. This would mean a wood in general use, with unrestricted access.

SLACK HEAD
Head of a valley, from ON slakki, and ON hofuð.

SLAGGYBURN
Boggy stream, from ON slagi 'damp,wet', and OE burna or ON brunnr.

SLEA GILL
Wet ravine, from ON slagi and ON gil.

SLEALANDS
Wet lands, from ON slagi and ON land.

SLEDDALE
Valley with a flat expanse of land, from ON sletta and ON dalr.

SLEETBECKS
Streams in a flat piece of land, from ON sletta and ON bekkr.

SLEIGHTHOLME
Island in a flat expanse of land, from ON sletta and ON holmr.

SMAITHWAITE
Either narrow clearing, or Smar's clearing, from ON smar, and ON thveit.

SNITTLEGARTH
This appears to mean 'enclosure where snares were set', from a dialect word 'snittle' 'noose type of snare' and ON garðr.

SOLWAY FIRTH
An early from Sulewad 1229 shows the second element to be ON vaðr 'ford'. The first element is obscure but could be OE sol 'muddy place', ON sul 'large stone', or even sula 'Solan goose'. The most likely explanation is ON sul referring to the Lochmaben Stone, a large ice-borne granite boulder which marked the Scottish end of the ford and was a recognised place for settling border disputes. Firth is from ON fjorðr 'fjord' or 'deep creek'.

SOULBY
Suli's home. This is likely to be a Danish name with the second element being Old Danish by.

SOUTERGATE
Sheep road, from ON sauðr 'sheep' in the plural sauðar, and ON gata. There is an ON word sutari meaning a shoemaker but the first explanation seems more likely.

SOUTERSTEAD
Place for sheep, from ON sauðr 'sheep' in the plural sauðar, and OE stede. There is a possibility that it could mean shoemaker's place from ON sutari as above.

SOUTHWAITE
An early form Sourthwaite recorded in 1360 shows that this name means clearing with muddy or poor soil, from ON saurr and ON thveit.

SOWERBY
Farm with muddy or poor soil, from ON saurr and ON byr.

SOW HOW
Pig hill, from either OE su and OE hoh or ON syr and ON haugr.

SPARK BRIDGE
No early forms but possibly from ON sprek 'dry twig', or 'brushwood', and OE brycg.

SPRINKLING TARN
In the 13th century this tarn was known as Prentibiountern. This seems to represent Prenti, or branded, Bjorn, an outlaw branded for his crimes living in a remote place. This had become Sparkling Tarn by 1774. The present name is modern.

ST BEES HEAD
Promontory of St. Bega, an Irish saint. The priory founded here in about 1125 was dedicated to Bega, an Irish virgin saint mentioned by Bede in the 7th century. The story is that she was of high birth and ran away from her father in Ireland to Cumbria to escape an arranged marriage. An alternative explanation could be that the name comes from Sancta Bega, meaning holy ring. In the church here up to the 13th century, a Norse silver arm ring was kept and used for oath swearing. The ancient name of this sandstone cliff was Baruth, from Irish barr ruagh, meaning red headland.

STAFFIELD
Field with a pole or post, from ON stafr and feldr.

STAINBURN
Stony stream, from ON steinn and ON brunnr.

STAINGARTH
Stone enclosure or yard, from ON steinn and ON garðr.

STAINMORE
Stony moorland, from ON steinn and ON mor.

STAINTON
Stony hamlet, from ON steinn and ON tun. There are many places of this name, and the Stainton in Furness has many large stones visible on the green to this day.

STAIR
No very early forms, but it could be from OE staeger 'to climb', with the implication that this is a steep part (of path, hill), a rise.

STAKE PASS
No early forms but probably a pass on a steep hill from ON stakkr.

STANGER
This could have three meanings. Either stakes or poles used as landmarks, from the plural stangar of ON stong; corner with a pole, from stong and ON vra; or shieling with a pole, from stong and ON erg.

STANK
Pole used as a landmark, from ON stong.

STANWIX
Stone ways or roads, from ON steinn and the plural of ON vegr. This was a Roman station on Hadrian's Wall.

STAPLETON
Farm by a post or pillar, from OE or ON stapol and OE or ON tun.

STAVELEY
Wood where thick sticks grew, from OE staef 'stick' and leah 'sparse wood'. These would be a result of coppicing.

STENNERLEY
Either Steinarr's slope, or possibly stone shieling on a long slope, from ON steinn, erg, and hlið. It could also be long slope with stones from the plural of ON steinn, steinnar and hlið.

STENNERSKEUGH
Wood on stony ground, from ON steinnar and ON skogr.

STICKLE PIKE
Steep peak, from OE sticol and OE peac.

STICKS PASS
No early forms but possibly steep pass, from OE sticol, or a pass marked by sticks, from OE sticca.

STOCKDALE
Tree stump valley, perhaps referring to land clearance. There are many prehistoric remains on the moor here.

STOCKDALEWATH
Landmark in a valley by the ford, from ON stokkr and dalr and vaðr. ON stokkr can also mean a tree stump, as above.

STODDAH
Hill with a pole, from ON stodr and ON haugr. However, the name could mean enclosure for horses from OE stod 'herd of horses', 'stud', and OE haga 'hedge', 'enclosure'.

STONETHWAITE
Land cleared of stones, from ON steinn and ON thveit.

STORRS
Woods, from ON storð.

STORTH
Wood, from ON storð.

STRICKLAND
Land for young bullocks or heifers, from OE styrc and OE land. There is a Strickland Ketel, from an ON personal name Ketil, and a Strickland Roger who was possibly Roger de Brounolfshefed, who had land there in 1340.

STRIDING EDGE
No early forms, but probably this name is from OE stridan with the now obsolete meaning of 'to straddle'. Edge is from OE ecg or ON egg 'sharp side of a blade'.

ST SUNDAY CRAG
St. Dominic's crag, from the Latin Dies Dominica 'the Lord's day', or Sunday.

STUDHOLME
Island or water meadow with a pole from ON stong and ON holmr. No early forms so this is a probable deduction.

STYHEAD
Top of the steep path, from ON stigr 'a steep path', and ON hofuð or OE heafod.

SUBBERTHWAITE
Either Suli's farm in a clearing, from ON Suli, erg, and thveit, or clearing by the muddy farm, from ON sul, ON byr and ON thveit.

SUNBRICK
Pigs' slope, from ON svin and brekka, as is shown from an early form Swynebrok 1269. Near this hamlet on Birkrigg Common is the site of a 17th century Quaker cemetery, which is not far from Swarthmoor Hall, where George Fox stayed frequently. He eventually married the owner's widow, Margaret Fell. Swarthmoor Hall became the centre of Quakerism.

SUNDERLAND
Land apart or separate land either in the sense of private land or land divided by a river, from OE sundorland.

SWAINSTEADS
Probably shepherd or farmhand's place, from ON sveinn and ON staðr, or OE stede. The first element could also be a Norse personal name, Sveinn.

SWARTHMOOR
The earliest recording of this name seems to be Swartemore 1537, which means black moor from OE blaec, or ON blakkr, and OE or ON mor. General Swartz camped here with 2000 Flemish troops supporting the attempt by Lambert Simnel on the throne of England in 1487. Domesday Book shows 'Warte' near this place, which could show there was a beacon here, from ON varðr.

SWEDEN BRIDGE
Land cleared by burning from ME swidden from OE sviða, and OE brycg.

SWINDALE
Pig valley, from ON svin and ON dalr.

SWINSIDE
Summer pasture where pigs were kept, from ON svin and ON saetr.

SWIRRAL HOWE
No early forms but could be from OE swira or ON sviri 'neck', 'col'. Howe is ON haugr 'hill'.

T

TALKIN
Probably 'white brow or end', from Celtic tal 'brow' or 'end', and Celtic cain 'white'. There is here a prominent hill with an outcrop on the summit of white rocks, either bleached sandstone or limestone which gives the village its name.

TALLENTIRE
End of the land, possibly referring to the high ground of the Lake District, from Celtic tal 'end', en 'the' and tir 'land'. The place is situated on flat land to the north of Cockermouth.

TARN HOWS
Small lake surrounded by hills, from ON tjorn and ON haugr. Although this is a comparatively modern dam, formed from damming three small tarns, the name was recorded in 1538.

TARNMONATH
Tarn by the hill, from ON tjorn and Celtic mynydd 'hill'.

TEBAY
Early forms Tibeia, 1179, and Tibbay c.1200, seem to indicate that the first element is probably a personal name Tiba and the second ON ey 'island'. Three streams meet at this point.

TEMPLE SOWERBY
Temple means belonging to the Order of the Knights Templar. Sowerby means farm with muddy or poor soil, from ON saurr and ON byr.

TERCROSSET
Thorgeirr's shieling, the last element being ON ergh, the first a Norse personal name.

TEWIT TARN
Peewit tarn. Tewit is the northern dialect word for peewit.

THACKMIRE
Swampy land where reeds for thatching grew, from ON thak and ON myrr.

THACKTHWAITE
Portion of land providing thatch, that is, coarse grass, rushes, or even bark, from ON thak and ON thveit.

THIRLMERE
The meaning is obscure. The earliest form seems to be Thyrlemere, 1574, so it could be lake in a hollow, from OE thyrel 'hollow'. However, the first element could be an ON personal name Thorhallr. The valley was known as Wythburn and the lake as Leatheswater before the 18th century. The water level was raised in the 19th century by Manchester Waterworks and is now a reservoir.

THIRLSPOT
From an early form, Thirspot 1616, it seems likely that this means giant's pool, from ON thurs and ON pot, with the 'l' being later inserted by analogy with nearby Thirlmere. Fisher Gill, immediately behind this hamlet, falls spectacularly into a series of deep pools.

THORFINSTY
Thorfinn's path, the second element being ON stigr, and the first a Norse personal name.

THORNBY
Either Thorunn's home, a feminine name, or home by the thorn tree. Some of the early forms quote Forneby, 1285, and Formeby, 1322, which suggests that the first element could be from ON forn, 'old', so the name could mean old home.

THORNY SCALE
Hut belonging to Thorny, an ON feminine personal name, and ON skali meaning hut.

THORNYTHWAITE
Clearing belonging to Thorny, or clearing in thorn trees, the second element being ON thveit.

THRANG GAP
Narrow gap, from ON throngr, and ON gapa.

THREAPLAND
Disputed land. The first element is ME threpen from OE threapian 'to contend'.

THRELKELD
Serf or bondman's well or spring, from ON thraell and ON kelda. It is thought that some Norwegians brought servants over from Ireland.

THRESHTHWAITE
There are no early forms but the meaning is probably 'clearing where threshing was done', from ON threskja and ON thveit.

THRIMBY
Either Thorunn, or Thyrne's home, or home by the thorn bush, from ON thyrnir and byr.

THRINGILL
Thorn bush ravine, from ON thyrnir and ON gil.

THUNACAR KNOTT
Hill belonging to Thorgeirr from an ON personal name and ON haugr. The second word is OE cnotta.

THUNDERSTONE
There are several rocks of this name in Cumbria. The early Modern English word 'thunder' referred to fossils, meteorites or large isolated stones usually used as boundary marks.

THURSBY
Thorir's home, from an ON personal name and ON byr or Old Danish by.

THURSTON WATER
Thorsteinn's lake. This is the old name for Coniston Water.

THWAITE FLAT
Clearing with a sheet of water, from ON thveit and ON fljot.

TILBERTHWAITE
The clearing by Tilli's fort. The first recording of this is Tildersburgthwait, 1196, showing the middle element to be OE burg, or ON borg, 'fort'. It is not known whether the fort was British or Roman. The last element is ON thveit.

TINDALE
Probably 'valley of the river Tyne'. Tyne is a British name meaning river, from the root ti- 'to flow'.

TIRRIL
Early form Tyrerhge 1189, shows the second element to be ON erg 'shieling'. The first element could be ON tyri 'dry wood'. So the name could mean 'shieling for or of dry wood'.

TOCK HOW
Toki's hill, the second element being ON haugr, and the first an ON personal name.

TOD GHYLL
Possibly fox ravine, from ME tod meaning fox. The second word is ON gil.

TODHILLS
Fox hills, from ME tod and ME hill.

TORPENHOW
Probably Thorfinnr's hill or burial mound, from an ON personal name and ON haugr. The entry in the EPNS volume on this area of Cumberland explains this name as main hill hill, from a presumed Celtic word torpen 'main hill' with ON haugr as a third element. As there is no hill at this village in north Cumbria it seems unlikely that this is the correct explanation.

TORVER
Torfi's shieling, from an ON personal name and ON erg. However, there is an ON word torfa meaning turf or peat, so the name could mean summer hut made of sods.

TOTTLEBANK
A lookout hill, from OE totian 'to peep out'. The second element is from ON banki.

TRIERMAIN
The early forms Trewermain, Treverman, 1200, suggest 'homestead at the stone', from Celtic tref yr maen.

TRINKELD
Thrandr's well, the second element being ON keldr, and the first a Norse personal name.

TROUTBECK
Trout stream. The first element is late OE truht from late Latin tructa. The second element is ON bekkr.

U

ULCAT ROW
Owl cottage corner, from OE ule-cot to which ON vra 'corner' was added later.

ULDALE
Ulfr's valley. 'Ulfr' is a personal name and also means a wolf in ON, so the place name could mean wolf valley.

ULGILL
Ulfr or wolf's ravine. The second element is ON gil.

ULLOCK
Wolves' playing place from ON ulfa and ON leikr.

ULLSWATER
Ulfr's lake. The second element is ON vatn later influenced by OE waeter which becomes ME water.

ULPHA
Either wolf hill or Ulfr's hill. The second element is ON haugr.

ULVERSTON
Ulfarr's farm, the second element being ON or OE tun, and the first a Norse personal name.

Signpost in Cartmel village. Hampsfield Fell is in the background.

UNTHANK
'Without permission'. This refers to a squatter's farm, and is from OE unthances.

URSWICK
There has never been a satisfactory explanation of this name. Eilert Ekwall suggested 'bison lake farm' from OE urs sae wic and this has been repeated by others. Another theory could be 'ore village' from OE ar, or OE ora, possibly in the genitive singular, ars, and OE wic. This may have been influenced by an earlier, Latin, aes vicus, the first element being similar in both languages. The reasons for suggesting this are as follows. The Iron Age shows that iron was mined 2500 years ago, at least. Furness is well known for its high quality haematite that has been mined for centuries. Most of these workings have now filled with water and become natural looking tarns. Iron ore is present near Urswick as the red colour of the soil on the valley floor shows. The water in Urswick Tarn is of a red hue. Ancient tumuli, settlements, homesteads and a fort show the area to have been inhabited for many hundreds of years. There is a local legend that 'a village' was swallowed by the waters of the tarn. That iron ore could have been mined by the Romans as well as the Britons is a tenuous theory based on the fact that most names ending in -wick in Cumbria are on Roman roads. Urswick is half a mile south of an ancient road called The Street, known locally as Red Lane, which links the main iron ore workings between Conishead, the entry to Furness over the sands, to Roanhead. A Roman coin, tripod and brass urn have been found in Urswick. Colonists usually plunder minerals to send to their native land. Other names show mine workings, such as Orgrave and Orton.

USKDALE
The valley of the river Isca, which is a British name meaning water. The second element is ON dalr.

UZZICAR
House in a field, from OE hus and OE aecer. This name has developed from Husaker, which was the name of a tarn, now drained, in the Newlands Valley.

W

WABERTHWAITE
Clearing by the hunting or fishing shed, from ON veiðibuð and ON thveit. Veiði means hunting or fishing, and buð means shed.

WALLA CRAG
Hill of the British, from OE walh in the genitive plural walla and OE hlaew. This fell is not far from the stone circle of Castlerigg near Keswick.

WALLENRIGG
No early forms but as this place occurs in an area of Celtic occupation on Broughton Common it is likely to mean 'ridge of the British', from ON val in the genitive plural valna, and ON hryggr.

WALLOWBARROW
No early forms, but probably 'hill of the British', from OE walh genitive plural walla and OE hlaew. Barrow 'tumulus' or 'mound', from OE beorg would have been added later.

WALNA SCAR
No early forms but perhaps this means 'hill of the British' from ON val in the genitive plural valna, and ON haugr. There are remains of many British settlements on both sides of this mountain. It was misinterpreted by early cartographers and written as Walney Scar on maps. Scar means rock or crag from ME skerre from ON sker 'low reef'.

WALNEY
It seems likely that this island was called different names by different people. There is evidence to show that it was larger than it is now, forested, and during the Middle Ages protected by a sea wall along its southern end. The Celts probably had a name for it now lost. To the Old English it was known as Wagneia 1127, probably meaning 'island of quicksands' which are still obvious in Morecambe Bay to the south and the Duddon estuary to the north. It was also probably the Houganai of Domesday Book, 'island of Hougun', another name for Furness in the 11th century. The name that has survived today is ON Valna ey, 'island of the Britons', and there are remains of an Iron Age bloomery at the northern end. Other proposals for the meaning of this name have been 'walled island' and even 'grampus island'.

WALTHWAITE
Clearing by a wall, from ON valr and ON thveit. It is possible that the name could mean 'clearing of the British', with ON val as first element.

WALTON
Farm on the wall, from OE weal and OE tun. This place-name is on Hadrian's Wall. There was another Walton in Furness, now lost, which would probably have meant 'farm of the British', from OE walh and OE tun.

WANSFELL
No early forms, but it could be Woden's fell named after one of the Norse gods. Another possibility is hunting ground, from ON van 'hunting ground' or 'a track that leads to hunting ground'. A third proposal is that the first element is from OE waegn 'waggon'. There are a number of broad old pathways such as Nanny Lane and Hundreds Lane leading up this fell, and a possible Roman road along the foot, maybe connecting the Roman fort at Ambleside with the Roman road which runs up Troutbeck.

WARCOP
Beacon hill, from OE weard or ON varða 'beacon' and OE copp 'hill'.

WARTH
There are no early forms but it seems likely to mean beacon from ON varða.

WARTHOLE
Beacon hill, from ON varða and ON haugr.

WARWICK
An early form Warthwic 1132, shows the name to mean 'farm by the beacon', from ON varða and OE wic. It is on a Roman road, east of Carlisle.

WASDALE
Valley of the lake, from ON vatn 'water' in the genitive vatns, and ON dalr.

WASTWATER
Apparently a contraction of Wasdale Water, so the meaning is 'lake of the valley of the lake'.

WATENDLATH
Barn by the end of the water, from ON vatn, ON endi and ON hlaða 'barn'.

WATERMILLOCK
An early form Wethermeloc shows that the first element is ON veðr 'sheep', and the second element a diminutive of Celtic moel 'hill' as in 'hillock'.

WATERYEAT
Water gate, from OE waeter and OE geat.

WATH
Ford, from ON vaðr. This hamlet is situated on the upper reach of the river Lune.

WATH SUTTON
The ford by the southern farm from OE or ON suðtun and ON vaðr.

WEASDALE
Probably weasel valley, from OE wesule and OE dael.

WESCOW
West wood, or hill. The early forms indicate either of these, from ON vestr and ON haugr or ON skogr. The hamlet is west of Threlkeld, near Keswick, and would seem to indicate that the thralls, or servants, were Norse speakers.

WESTMORLAND
This former county name disappeared in 1974 when Cumbria was formed. The early form Westmoringaland 1150 shows it to mean 'land of the people who live on the western moors', obviously used by those living on the east side of the Pennines.

WESTRAY
Western corner, from ON vestr and ON vra.

WETHERAL
Corner where sheep were kept, from OE wether and OE halh.

WETHERLAM
There are no early forms so the etymology is dubious. The first element could be ON veðr or OE wether 'sheep'. The second element could be OE lam 'soil' or OE or ON land.

WHALE
Early forms Qwalle 1278 and Qwale 1345 show this word to be from ON hvall 'round hill'.

WHALLO
There are no early forms but it is likely to be round hill, from ON hvall and ON haugr. There is a possibility that it could mean 'hill of the British', from OE walh or ON val 'Briton' and ON haugr 'hill'. In an unstressed position haugr becomes -o in place-names.

WHARRELS HILL
Hill with (stone) circles from OE hweol 'wheel'.

WHARTON HALL
An early form Werfton, 1202, shows this place to mean farm on the

embankment, from OE hwerf and OE tun. It is on the river Eden. The name has been transferred to the moor behind.

WHASSET
There are no early forms but the name probably means shieling on a hill, from ON haugr and ON saetr.

WHEELBARROW
Hill of the stone circle, from OE hweol 'wheel or circle' and OE beorg 'hill'. An alternative meaning could be circular burial mound from the same elements. Compare Kirkbarrow.

WHELPO
Hvelpr's hill, the second element being ON haugr, and the first a Norse personal name.

WHELP RIGG
Hvelpr's ridge. As well as being a personal name, ON hvelpr means 'cub'.

WHERNSIDE
Hillside where millstones were obtained, from OE cweorn-side.

WHILLAN BECK
This is probably a personal name Willan, and ON bekkr.

WHILLIMOOR
Wheel moor, perhaps referring to stone circles, from OE hweol 'wheel or circle' and OE mor.

WHINLATTER
Animals' lairs surrounded by furze bushes, from a ME word whin 'furze' probably of Scandinavian origin. The second element is ON latar 'animals' lairs'.

WHITBARROW
White hill, from ON hvita or OE hwit and ON berg or OE beorg. This is a prominent limestone hill east of the Lyth valley.

WHITBECK
White stream, from ON hvita and ON bekkr. There are two waterfalls cascading down the slope of Black Combe which give this hamlet its name.

WHITEHAVEN
White headland harbour, from ON hvita, ON hofuð, and ON hafn.

WIGTON
Wicga's farm, an OE personal name and OE or ON tun.

WINDER
Shieling or shelter in a windy place, from ON vindr and ON erg.

WINDERMERE
Vinand's lake from an Old Scandinavian personal name and OE mere. The town of Windermere developed only after the arrival of the railway in 1847. Prior to that it was a hamlet called Birthwaite 'clearing in the birch trees', from ON birkr and ON thveit.

WINDERWATH
Vinand's ford, from an ON personal name and ON vaðr 'ford'.

WINSCALE
A hut used for shelter against the wind, from ON vindr and ON skali.

WINSKILL
The early form Wynscales 1292 shows the meaning to be the same as Winscale.

WINSTER
The river Winster means the left river, from ON vinstri meaning left. It is in contrast to the rivers Leven and Gilpin which are on the right of the valley looking north.

WINSTER
The village Winster also means the left one but another element, thwaite 'clearing' has been lost from the modern name.

WINTON
Possibly windy farm, from OE wind and OE tun.

WITHERSLACK
Wooded valley, from ON viðr and ON slakki.

WORKINGTON
Farm of the descendants of Wirc, an OE personal name. OE ingaton means 'home of the descendants'.

WREAY
Corner, from ON vra. This tiny hamlet nestles in the crook of a hillside near Ullswater. There are other names in Cumbria, Wray, Wrea, from the same element.

WRYNOSE PASS
Stallion's neck pass from ON vreini and ON hals.

WYTHBURN
This place-name was used for the whole of Thirlmere valley. Old forms Withebotine 1280 and Wythebodin 1303 show the probable meaning to be 'wood in a valley', from ON viðr and ON botn. The first element could be 'willow trees', from ON viðir, however. The second element changed to 'burn' in the 17th century.

WYTHOP
Either willow valley, from OE withe and OE hop, or wood in a valley, from ON viðr.

Y

YANWATH
Early forms Euenwith 1150 and Yafnewid 1245 seem to indicate that this name means 'flat wood', from ON jafn and ON viðr. However, as this place stands on the river Eamont it is more likely that the name means Eamont ford, the first element being a contraction of the river name and the second ON vaðr 'ford'.

YARLSIDE
Chieftain's shieling, from ON jarl 'earl' and ON saetr.

YEORTON
ON Iofurr's farm, or OE Eofor. As well as being a personal name this also means wild boar.

YEWDALE
Valley with yew trees, from OE iw or ON yr and ON dalr.

YOKE
No early forms but could be an ON personal name Iokull, or 'lower' from Gaelic iochdar. This hill is 100 feet lower than its neighbour Ill Bell.

Select Bibliography

Barnes, F. *Barrow and District*, Barrow 1951.

Bulmer, T.(ed.) *History Topography and Directory of Furness and Cartmel*, Preston (undated).

Collingwood, W.G. *Lake District History*, Kendal 1925.

Collingwood, W.G. *The Lake Counties, revised by William Rollinson*, London 1988.

Darton, Mike *The Dictionary of Scottish Place-Names*, Moffatt 1990.

Ekwall, Eilert *Oxford Dictionary of English Place Names*, 4th Ed., Oxford 1960.

Ekwall, Eilert *The Place-Names of Lancashire*, Manchester 1922.

Ellis, Peter Berresford *Celtic Inheritance*, London 1992.

Ellis, Peter Berresford *The Celtic Empire. The First Millenium of Celtic History c.1000BC to 51AD*, London 1990.

Ellis, Peter Berresford *Celt and Saxon-The Struggle for Britain AD410-937*, London 1993.

English Place-Name Society *English Place-Name Elements*, Cambridge 1956.
Place-Names of Cumberland, Cambridge 1950.
Place-Names of Westmorland, Cambridge 1967.

Gambles, Robert *Lake District Place-Names*, Kendal 1985.

Gelling, Margaret *Signposts to the Past*, London 1988.

Kelly, Joan *Scandinavian Elements in North West Place Names*, Unpublished thesis Liverpool University 1961.

Lindqvist, Harald *Middle English Place Names of Scandinavian Origin*, Uppsala 1911.

Mills, A.D. *A Dictionary of English Place-names*, Oxford 1991.

Mills, David *The Place Names of Lancashire*, London 1986.

Millward, R. and Robinson, A. *The Lake District*, London 1974.

Ordnance Survey Placenames on Maps of Scotland and Wales, Southampton 1981.

Rask, R.C. A Grammar of the Icelandic or Old Norse Tongue translated from Swedish by GW Dasent, London, Frankfurt, 1843, ed. TL Markey, Amsterdam, 1976.

Rollinson, William   A History of Cumberland and Westmorland, Sussex 1978.

Room, A.   Dictionary of Place-names in the British Isles, London 1988.

Scott, J. A Lakeland Valley through Time, Kendal 1995.

Sedgefield, W.J. Place Names of Cumberland and Westmorland, Kendal 1915.

Shotter, David   Romans and Britons in North West England, Lancaster 1993.

The Collins Spurrell Welsh Dictionary, London and Glasgow 1987.

The Oxford Dictionary of English Etymology, Oxford 1966.

Transactions of the Cumberland and Westmorland Antiquarian Society.

Waterhouse, John   The Stone Circles of Cumbria, Cambridge 1985.

West, Thomas   Antiquities of Furness, 'new edition' with additions by W Close, Ulverston 1805.

Wyld, H.C. and Hirst, T.O.   The Place-Names of Lancashire, London 1911.

About the Author

Joan Lee read English at the University of Liverpool from 1958 to 1961. This entailed learning Old Norse, Gothic, Old English with its several dialects, and Middle English. Her interest in place-names was kindled whilst researching for her thesis 'Scandinavian Elements in North West Place-Names', which has provided the basis for this book. She became a teacher of English and Latin but worked on a part time basis after the birth of her children. She has lived in many parts of the world accompanying her husband in his work. She wrote short stories for the radio while living in Oman, and started work on Cumbrian place-names on her return from India in 1993.